Rosemarie F Elrod
2016

Born Into Chaos

A Memoir: 1941 to 1964

ROSEMARIE FLORECK ELROD

Printed in the United States of America

First Printing, 2015

ISBN-10: 0989839257
ISBN-13: 978-0-9898392-5-9

DEDICATION

To my son, James Philip Elrod Jr. and my grandchildren

Ashley Nicole Elrod and James Kelly Elrod

And great-grandson Ryane

IN MEMORY

My mother, Anna Floreck, my father, Heinz Haase,

My grandparents, Karl Floreck and Marie Virginie Schoenahl Floreck

And the rest of the bunch,

Without them I would not have become who I am.

Contents

ACKNOWLEDGEMENTS

Thanks to my friend John L Warren III

and my childhood friend, George Frieler in Epe, Germany

for their help and encouragement.

Chapter 1

Born Into Chaos

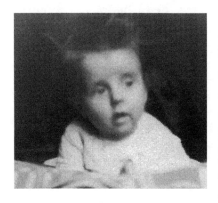 August 1941 so it begins. I am born into chaos. The bombs detonated all around us rubble, distraction and I am in the middle of it, in Cologne. What a beginning. Mother gave birth in a hospital to which grandmother had walked her, just minutes earlier. I was half out before the nurses where rounded up to help her. She weighed 88 pounds. My father was missing somewhere in WWII, not returning after his last mission, and she was not married to him. Every night the siren went off and we rushed, with already packed suitcases and important papers into the nearest Bomb Shelter.

My mother was shunned for having a baby and not being married. They could have had a telephone wedding, but my father wanted the 2 week's leave that was norm in war time when getting married. He was to go on one more mission before the leave to get married. He never returned, was never found, not one trace of him. We searched by Red Cross for years. On Saturdays, his name was called out on the Official Radio Station. They were reading names of parents looking for children, those separated during the nightly bombing attack, running to get into the shelter; those who had gotten lost on the long trek from east to west. Children looking for their parents, those old enough to know their names. Then the description of children that could only be identified by the clothes they had worn, approximate age and where found when separated. Some had notes and name tags pinned on them with information. Those were the lucky ones. Then came the names of soldiers. It seemed never-ending.

If my father could have married my mother, in whatever way, her family would have forgiven her. Indiscretions did happen; just don't get caught. It did not matter that Heinz, my father, was introduced and so placed right into the circle of mom's life by her older brothers who knew him.

She was 19 years old when she met him. Heinz, Officer of an Elite Unit, was attached to the *"Luftwaffe"* (German Air Force). They talked to each other in hushed voices, sharing secrets about missions, sometimes right here in Germany, speculating. Some of his missions, at home, were to join the festivities or accompany high ranking staff members.

A special program had started, in absolute secret, where pregnant, single women gave birth. They were supervised under doctors and nurses care, supplied with good, healthy food, clean living and this in war times where everything was scarce. Not in those places, he told his comrades; they had everything they needed.

The fathers of the babies were unknown. It was whispered that they were high officials, clean Aryans. After birth the children were placed into certain SS families to be raised as their own. This special program was to revitalize the German race, create a "Master Race." Families were in general encouraged to have upwards of five children. Heinz knew things; they all tried to speculate what it was all about. Lots of soldiers, having been put in close vicinity, tried to get in on that action if they could. If found out, they were transferred. Sex,

2

illiteracy and promiscuity was made OK at the highest level as long as you picked a desirable partner. Nobody really knew what this was all about at that time. Later it became known, but ever so slowly. It had been a secret too long hidden from view.

My mom fell instantly in love with my father. He was so dashing, she tells me. When his unit was called up, they took leave of each other. They made love. One time only. That's all it took to create me. It seems not possible, but I am the proof. He was sent out on one more mission with the choice of marriage by phone, right then, or after he returned. He chose the two weeks. Who could know he would not come back, dead, missing in action. Mother was alone, shunned, trying to hide her ever growing belly, with plans to adopt me out, to somebody on grandfather's side of the family in Berlin.

Nothing was ever the same. Mother went off to Berlin to sit out the pregnancy and to have me adopted. Nobody should know, should find out. It was OK for men, but not for women. Most of my uncles had children out of wedlock. Grandfather had one for which he paid until the child was 18 years old; nobody ever talked about it. I found out, somehow! My mom compared all men to my father. Who could stand up to the hero, missing in action? There was hope he might come back, broken, disheveled but still alive. However, it was not to be.

I remember mother wanted to learn typing, but it was in the next town over so they feared for her safety and did not let her go. Similar with learning to fix hair. She told me often. When I asked, "MOM, why did you not just insist on it," she shrugged her shoulders and gave me a sad look. "I could not stand up for myself." This was always her answer. It made me angry every time she said it. Of course, not all Germans thought this way but a pretty big bunch did, especially in the rural areas and also the Germans that were not highly educated, which meant a great mass of people.

Well, the times were changing and the old systems nearly gone with no norms on how things were supposed to be done. The old days were gone! Nothing happened the way they thought. Yet my elders were stuck in that old system.

Nobody had time or the inclination to take care of a sister without a husband. She needed to learn to fend for herself. They expected my mother to, but did not really give her the proper chance. They just imposed their will and mother was not strong enough to go up against them; she got dominated, wailed against it, yes, then did not stand up to them. People were shell-shocked and it went on like that for a long time.

Did her brothers or even grandma try to help her? They did, I think, but who knows? They helped by taking mother back and by taking me on.   Uncle Karl made sure there was no longer any talk of adopting me out. He would not hear of it and told my mother he would help raise me.   Then grandmother took over at some time after that; she always did. Mother went back to the business of being a young person. She was 20 years old.

While my mom was in Berlin, waiting for me to show up, she got scared hearing rumors about the behavior of Russian soldiers. People still remembered WW I. I think, however, that she just did not want to be alone, giving birth, away from grandma. Air raids were over Berlin just as well as over Cologne. She went home. There she waited inside a park, highly pregnant, for it to be dark so she could slip back into her mother's house, unseen. I don't think she ever forgave grandmother for making her wait in the park for the cover of darkness.

Grandmother dominated her, but she dominated all the others as well. Grandma told mother what to do. She just did not take a stand. Grandfather or Uncle Karl intervened for her. I think that it was easy to let them take charge, as they always had before. They were in a war, somebody had to take charge, so grandmother did.

Later on, when I was older and my uncles continued to dominate mother, unjustified, I hated them. They came back, my father did not. It was not fair. In that time, it seemed that mother somehow slipped into the position of an older sister. I called her Mutti, which was the equal to mommy and I called my grandmother, Oma. The old power structure had re-established itself in my small family. Mother held the position of an older sister.

It took a while for me to be feisty enough to fight my mother's battles, mouthing off, confronting my uncles, and sometimes grandmother, when they all made slighting remarks about her dating attempts or about her boyfriends.

At school I feared the kids, hinting at irregularities of my birth, about my father, whose name I did not have. I was lucky; kids were basically too naive to understand what they had overheard. Gossip and speculation did not make them any smarter, but I started to ask questions at home.

I swung around admiring my uncles often enough, at other times. They were not all bad, just so typically German. I listened to their stories, the places they went and the interesting lives they seemed to live, all these war stories. Were they true, or made up? Did they embellish them? The liberties they took. None granted to my mother. At times they made me angry enough, then I would go after them because I knew their secrets.

If she had secured a new husband, it would have been different. I wanted her to find one because that would have given me sisters and brothers, maybe. I found out later, when I understood such matters, that many did not live up to mom's expectations or grandmas for that matter. That was the end of it. There were several real decent men that had asked her to marry, and they would have adopted me as well. Mother was very good looking, with big brown eyes from our French side. This line included wine farmers, like Great Grandmother Virginia from around Strasbourg. My mother was always talked out of marriage by her family. I contributed my uncle's objection to the fact that they knew things the rest of the family did not. I did not either and never could find out, no matter how much I was digging, until much later.

There was now confusion about my father. Had they really known him at all? Little by little things come out. Of course, facts were hidden. Everywhere facts were hidden. You would ask questions and, if you did, you got no answers. Grandma Marie did not know anything. I heard that they often kept things from her.

Then we were hit with the paper work and the knowledge that two more women had been looking for my father. One lived in Hamburg; one somewhere in East Germany; then us, in Cologne, which was his hometown. Then, inside the family, the speculation started again. Who the heck was he and how come nothing was found out about him, his mission, the plane or his comrades.

Could he have taken off to places unknown, like some of Uncle Ernst's superiors at the end of the war? But his father, Grandfather Haase, had not heard from him either but got notification that he had been missing in action and now believed he was killed on that last mission.

Mother had been visiting Grandfather Haase, off and on for information until he himself got killed in a raid. They had fighter planes shooting at people in the streets. He was not fast enough to get out of the streetcar. A bullet hit him and that was the end of that side of the family. They are all dead. There was no family left on my father's side.

Many years later, when all the paperwork came together, it was revealed that two more women also had children and were looking for him. All I ever was able to find out was that these children were girls. No matter how we came to be. All my life I have wished I could have known them.

Chapter 2

Life Under Air Raids

When the sirens went off, I was transported back and forth inside a huge soft feather pillow that we called a puff puff. At night I was put fully clothed into an oversized dresser drawer, ready to be grabbed in a hurry to run off to the nearest bomb shelter. There was no crib for me. I was 3 months old.

One of these nights, grandfather had the job to grab me and put me inside the pillow and proceed to the shelter, while grandma, mama and Uncle Karl followed with suitcases, one in each hand. The suitcases were pre-packed, ready to go by the first sign of alarm. One never knew what was left standing after the air raid.

On this particular night a bomb came down very close. Detonation and the "*Luftdruck*" (shockwave) were tremendous, scared the heck

9

out of grandfather and by the time he got to the shelter, he had an empty puff puff in his arms. He had lost me. I had slipped out somehow and he did not notice it.

Good grief, that was a scary situation. Once in the shelter, where everyone was packed in like sardines, standing room only, my family was waiting to discover I was gone. Then words passed on that a man had just arrived up front, with a child, which was not his. He had been behind grandpa and had seen me slipping out. He dropped his other suitcase picked me up and continued running towards the shelter.

 The shelter was so packed that they had to come up with a creative way to reunite me with my folks. It was decided to pass me over the heads, over everybody's head, until I arrived back with mother. It was a very long, tunnel like shelter and grandmother remarked often, thereafter, that I had not uttered one whimper, not even a little whine. However, after that, grandfather was taken off the baby carrying duty. Grandmother took over and grandfather was demoted to suitcase's carrier. I don't think he was all that unhappy about it.

Grandmother loved telling these stories to me and I loved hearing them. She must have told them often; otherwise, I would not remember them so vividly and here is one of my favorite.

When I was 9 months, I walked and was potty trained. I don't know if this is really true or if they had trained themselves to know when I needed to go. However, everything was rationed and one had to request and had to prove why it was needed. There were regulations for everything, some kind of system in place and rationing cards.

Grandmother went to get shoes for me. I had been running around on self-knitted socks and there was little chance to keep them clean. She stood in line. Finally she got in to see the civil servant in charge. He looked at her and said, "How old and what size?" Grandma told him and he stopped flipping through his paperwork and told her; "My good woman, I don't know of any child that walks at 9 months!" "She walks and she needs them now," was grandma's replay.

"Really," he replied. "You want me to believe this? Do you have a birth certificate?" She produced it. Grandma always came prepared. It did not help her on this particular day. He just shook his head and told her, "I am sorry, children do not walk that early, per my regulations. Come back when she can."

Grandma took a deep breath, then told him, "I will be back." He grinned at her and waved an "*Auf Wiedersehen*" (goodbye), then he hollered out to the waiting crowd "Next!" She was back the next day, got in front of the long line, telling the waiting crowd, "I am expected" and she marched straight into his office, having me on her arm, stopped in front of his desk and plopped me on it. There I promptly got up on my wobbly, fat legs and started to walk all over his paper work.

He was a younger guy, at least at lot younger than grandmother, with a sense of humor, "Thank God," and he started laughing out loud and said, "OK...OK, you have convinced me." She left with the required paper to get a pair of shoes issued for me.

The next incident was about 1 1/2 years later when I got away from my Uncle Karl's tailor shop. I escaped when somebody left the door open and I went out down the steps, scooting down backwards from the 3rd floor and left the apartment building. My mother just happened to be on the balcony, facing the front street and saw me running down the main street and around the corner. By the time everybody was alerted, I was well gone and out of sight. Fortunately, the neighborhood bakery sales girl had spotted me and enticed me to come into her store with something sweet; that is when mom was able to collect me again. Even then I was always on my way to someplace.

Chapter 3

Uncle Herman in the Air Raid

Uncle Herman, mama's youngest brother, studied to be a *Schreiner* (carpenter) and went into the German Merchant Marines at 19 years of age. Boys who could not swim would be thrown overboard into the water. Either they learned in a hurry or they drowned. He enlisted in the Spanish War somewhere between 1936-1941. He volunteered. He wrote a bunch of letters dated them and left them with a friend to mail at per-arranged dates to his mother, my grandmother. She became suspicious when she received letters posted in the wrong order.

He did not want anybody to know that he had enlisted in a war he had no business participating in. I personally never figured out which side he was on. The International Brigade was in favor of helping the defense of Madrid. There was an early Battalion, German speaking and associated with or noted as the Weimar Republic's "lost generation" fighting to ward off fascism in a political struggle, which already had conquered most of Europe. Mr. Hitler was for Franco, who eventually turned out the winner, which was Nationalist. In a pure sense, they were recruited by Russia and were communists.

So Hitler was supporting General Franco and that would have made Uncle Hermann fight on the wrong side. However, I really think this is quite complicated; we never figured it out, who he was supporting,

and why. He came back wounded and had to fess up because the letters gave him away. His brothers huddled around him to come up with a plausible story as to how and where he was wounded.

He then winds up in Hitler's Navy on a U-boat. Maybe he did support the right side, meaning Hitler, because he seemed to have made it up the ranks quickly. It is said he was on the U-boat that ran down the Rhine River; for whatever reason, nobody really knew. This is not bloody likely.

He was always full of mischief and lots of shenanigans. An adventurer of some kind and he knew how to spin a sailor's yarn, together with Uncle Willie.

When they got back into the North Atlantic from the trip down the Rhine River, they ran into enemy fighters. The U-boat was floating on top of the water; why again, he just did not say. They did not spot

the fighter plane until they were fired on. That would have been the English from across the Channel. They had been on an unauthorized maneuver and they were drunk, the way he told it.

I heard him. I used to sneak in, hide under the dining table, listening to all of their stories. I was fascinated. What a life! Was he telling a lie, was he exaggerating, embellishing, or what? I kept myself still, making myself smaller then I was. I was not going to miss out on this story. He was wounded again at that time, that much is true, for sure. Since he never got court-marshaled, I figured he was on some kind of mission when it happened down the Rhine River, or not.

This time it took a while to fix him up. He was sent to a field hospital in the country. It took three quarters of a year to get him walking again. Then he came to Cologne to visit his mom and dad, my grandparents.

Meantime, there was a full-fledged war and air raids over Germany. He was out with some of his friends, also on leave, comrades, when he got caught up in an air raid which catapulted him straight across the street. He landed again in a hospital, this time a civilian hospital, with broken bones and internal injuries, while Cologne was bombarded every night.

He had been sitting out the war so far, being wounded, and now here he is back in the hospital. The only way he could get to a military field hospital, outside city limits, was to be in good enough shape for transportation. This was not the case.

He instructed my mother, his sister, to bring food and ice to drop his fever. They were only moving soldiers out that were not badly wounded. He was and he knew it. He told my mother, "They will not take me if I have a fever and if I stay here, I will die. This hospital is like a sitting duck."

I was wondering, where did she get the ice, war and all. I asked her a long time ago and she told me. There was a beer factory, close by. They had an ice machine, not for consumption but it was used to keep beer and other drinks cool. Would you not just know it, there was a beer factory, still standing and functioning and bombs detonating all around? Where there is a will, there is a way.

Mother trucked over there every day, put the ice into a warm water bottle, now cold water bottle, and packed her brother down. Usually it was put onto the groin area. Then there was the alcohol which was soaked into a cloth and then wrapped around his ankles. It was called "*Kalte Wadenwickel zum senken des Fiebers*" (cold ankle wraps). This was to lower the fever, as well. She was caught along the way with the alcohol and sent packing. The nurses investigated no further so his temperature stayed altered.

Well, that makes me think. I must have been born already, and this would have made it after 1941 because our house got bombed the first time, a direct hit, and split in half. It sank to one side.

The effort of keeping him cooled down, or somewhat normal, made him one of the soldiers that was transported out. Several days later, the same air raid, that took out our house, took the hospital. Everybody that had not been able to move into the shelter, under the hospital, was dead. My mom saved his life.

I don't recall he ever thanked her for it. By the time he got healed up, after all his broken bones healed (his hip, his legs) he was not much use as a soldier. He was no longer 100 percent, in some departments. I heard them talking about it. He had lost his first wife by now. Through all this rigmarole, she had not been faithful and turned up to be pregnant and he claimed it was not his. "That's life."

However, he had time to think about what was going on in Germany and started to make up his own mind. He told his brothers (I overheard this one, too) that he smartened up and took measures to stay alive, trying to stay out of the line of fire. He survived. He was smashed up, lost part of his hearing and considered himself "Quasi" a war hero, having been wounded twice, which netted him an extra high pension later, when he retired.

After the war, he became a union boss, was political for a while and went up that ladder as well. He gave me my first job at 15 years of age as his office helper in the time of summer vacation.

He found another wife, Aunt Grete, by all accounts a trophy wife.

 She worked for Britain's Occupation force in Osnabrueck. She was extremely likable. Very pretty, with dark brown hair, beautiful brown eyes, slender, sexy and liked man's attention, a lot of attention. Hence she worked for the Occupation Forces, where he found her.

There were not enough men to go around; too many had died. In order to get a fellow, you had to be not only pretty but also accomplished in the art of keeping the guy once you got him. She was. Grandma told me so.

Uncle Herman was no longer as virile, still young, but having been shot to pieces many times. He lost some of his stamina, again per grandma who seemed to be an expert on that subject. This is where the "not being 100 percent" came from, I finally figured it out.

Aunt Grete had been observed trying to obtain extra attention, especially when they partied and she could cover it up, "Oh, I just got a little bit too friendly." Under the guise of drunkenness, she even went for Uncle Willie whose new girlfriend was watching him like a hawk, being that he was not yet divorced from his first wife.

I know this, too, per my mother. If Grete had been in Epe while we were still living there on one of Uncle Willie's visits, he would have been more than tempted. He went after all of mom's girlfriends. To the point that mother had to warn them because she knew nothing would come of it. I know of that, too; it was one of my secrets, I knew about him! He was the meanest of my uncles. Aunt Grete was forever trying to get attention, even I noticed.

Back to Uncle Hermann who always forgave Aunt Grete. He minimized the incidents; he always believed her. She was worth it, and he took a "grin and bear" attitude about it.

He was a good catch, very handsome, had a very good job and, after all, what is a little bit of extra sex, anyway? (This per some of my German friends that held the same position). This was not my attitude but I had quite a few friends who surprised me on that account.

Chapter 4

Evacuation

Off to the train station, each of us allowed just one piece of language, a bag or box filled up with personal stuff. Even I had a small suitcase, which I dragged on the ground behind me. I am 3 1/2 years old. We are on our way to the relocation camp, being evacuated, because the house is bombed out, kaput, all gone.

The last air raid finished off the already damaged house. The basement had collapsed onto itself with us in it, and we had to dig out. The door to the outside was blocked by rubble. Before that, the house was just banged up. This last time we had been buried in the basement, when it partly collapsed. It was apparent, even to the city, our street was no longer safe. We were on the list to go, to be shipped off, to somewhere else.

I was told "hang on to that suitcase; do not let go" and so I did as I was told. I defended it with all my might. It was heavy and had more than just my clothes in it. When it came to being helped into the train, officials seeing to our peaceful departure, I got into trouble. I would not let go of my suitcase.

I refused to let go. I protested loudly. After all, I had packed the only doll I had into it. The one with the porcelain head which had a hole in it. All my dolls had holes in their heads. I would drop them on the floor, hence the hole. The rest of the body was stuffed with soft material. The official, at the station, regulating a huge amount of people finally had enough. He grabbed me, suitcase attached, and shuffled me into the train while he mumbled under his breath, *"Du kleiner Luemmel,"* (you little rascal).

We had to leave a lot behind, Oma said, and it's not the first time for her. She did not like it any better now. But we had our lives and it was promised that we would get relocated somewhere less devastated by the war. The war had not reached into some of the farmland; our destination was Epe, close to Holland. The State had ordered the farmers to house bombed-out families.

First, however, we are off to be assembled in a camp where people showed up from God knows where to get counted, checked out, deloused, registered and then sent off onto farms.

Grandfather was afraid we would get separated from each other, being stuffed into different compartments. He patrolled back and forth in good old German soldier manner to keep track of us. After all he was a soldier, a sergeant back in the first WW.

I don't remember the name of the camp but it was big and smelled of disinfectant. It looked like a huge gymnastic school stadium, fitted with hundreds of cots to sleep on, with one blanket. We got examined lightly, deloused and then assigned a cot. I watched this man in the white coat with this sharp thing in his hand. He was poking people with it. I did not like the looks of it. The people ahead made faces, too, and did not like it either. Also what was up with that bad smelling powder they put on my hair, this delousing

20

stuff got into my eyes; they were itchy and watering. It was just sprayed over us and missed most of the heads. They were in a hurry and so many people to spray.

When that man, in the white coat came closer, I started to fuss in anticipation. Oma said I had a nose for suspecting trouble. Then I would go into my *"Radau mode"* or, what we call here, I threw a tantrum until the trouble left me in a hurry. I did not stop hollering until grandmother came and shut me up. I don't remember if I got the shot or if they gave up. I do remember, however, that I did get every childhood disease that was around and came out of it just fine.

We had to leave Uncle Karl behind in Cologne. He died at the same time the house took a full hit and split in halve, sort of. Grandma almost got it, too. She was lucky. That night she had just made it back into the basement shelter from her outpost in the attic.

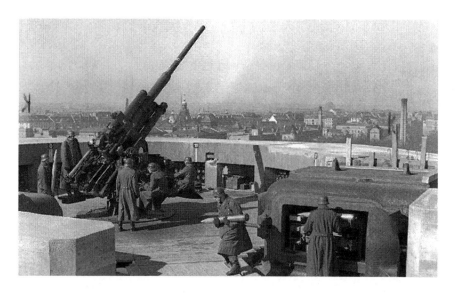

It was her habit when the air raids started to climb up and watch the *"Flak"* through the attic window and try to predict how close the bombs came. She watched the *"Flieger Abwehr Kanone"* (anti aircraft batteries) and often stayed to the last minute. She seemed to have figured out a system which told her how close they were and when to take off for the shelter; then she came down, to report.

That particular night she came down quickly and did not notice that Uncle Karl was not there. He had climbed up to check his shop for damage in between air raids. That night they took a long time to finish with us. One air raid wave followed another all night long. When it was over, they went up and found him. He was lying in front of his tailor shop on the 3rd floor, dead, with an unexploded bomb next to his head.

However, that was not what killed him. He was born with a weak heart, the eldest of grandma's children. He had been a breech birth which left him with a weak heart. He must have come out of his shop, when the house took another hit. The detonation and possibly the shock wave made his heart stop.

This was mom's second tragedy since my dad was missing in action. He was the one who stopped them, the family, trying to adopt me out to grandfather's family in Berlin. Now he was gone, too. We had to leave him behind. There was lots of confusion after that air raid on our street. People running all over the place, some digging out family buried alive, not yet dead or soon would be because of their injuries.

There were no functional funeral homes around. We had to keep Uncle Karl in one of the bedrooms until he could be picked up and buried. It took some time and I had been looking for my favorite uncle. The one that always played with me. Why was he taking a nap in the middle of day? I climbed up on the bed, started to shake him and when he did not wake up, I climbed onto him, sat on his chest and my little hands slapped his face gently to get him to wake up.

That is when they found me and hauled me off, lamenting that somebody had not locked that bedroom door. I protested, but to no avail. I never saw Uncle Karl again and found out very much later that he was gone forever.

I found a death notice later, in grandma's papers, which stated the following:

"In the night of April 20 to 21 in 1944 Karl Floreck died in the terror attack hurled onto the city of Koeln-Lindenthal. When it was over, he was dead of a heart attack."

They actually called it a terror attack. That is why I knew the exact date, when we lost him and when we were totally bombed out.

He was the one, the tailor, much adored by all the ladies because he made wonderful suits and dresses, as long as you brought the fabric, the material. He would make you a miracle dress or suit and he always had left over to outfit me and mom, his sister.

Because of him we did not go that hungry because he took food in trade for payment of the garments he made. But now we were on our way, alone, without him, to Epe and I would be living on a farm with animals. Imagine that, lots of animals like cows, pigs, chicken and dogs. I hoped for dogs.

Chapter 5

On the Farm

Finally we are there, on the farm, somewhere around Epe and it is a big one. It was run by two women. The old Mrs. Niemann, whose husband was dead and the young Miss Hedwig, whose husband was in the war, somewhere. They ran the farm with two very old ranch hands, doing the hard work, like plowing the fields. Mother and I were sent to them, *"Oma" and "Opa"* (grandparents) a few miles up the road on a different farm.

As soon as we arrived on the grounds, I got jumped on and nearly tumbled over by this white ball of fur, up and down he jumped in his excitement to greet me. A small white dog, a terrier, with a little brown on his nose and some on his pelt. He raced up, surrounded me barking and was absolutely excited to greet me. His name was *"Spitz."*

He was my very own greeting committee, Spitz, the terrier. He was a small dog, but what he did not have in size, he made up in enthusiasm. We, Spitz and I, were the smallest things around on this farm. I was sold on him. This was what I had hoped for.

We fell in love with each other from the start. I was never seen without him, close by. If they wanted to track me down, see what I was up to, they just needed to whistle for him. Where I was, Spitz was, or the other way around. He also responded when called or whistled for! I usually did not. I was too busy investigating and discovering this wonderful place called a farm.

They had all kinds of animals I had heard about. Chickens, cows, horses, pigs, rabbits, goats, cats and piglets. I watched Miss Hedwig milk the cows. She laughed when I wanted to try. She let me. The cow's tail kept swiping over my face and my little hands were not strong enough to get one drop of milk out. The cow hands were laughing, remarking that the cow did not like me trying to milk her. I should stop before she would use more then her tail to swipe me off. That is when they told me that Mathilde would have a baby, soon.

There was also a big old barnyard dog, a Shepherd, very old. He was not at all friendly and would not let me come close. He just took off and watched me from afar. His job was to patrol the ground, and he eyed me very suspiciously for a long time. He did not mind Spitz, but I could not get close to him without the grown-ups. There were always little animals being born, and I had to check each morning to see what new animal had arrived. It was a big job and it kept me busy.

My clean clothes, put on in the morning, did not stay clean long on my busy schedule, investigating the goings-ons. I wandered around the place, especially into all the stalls with the animals, petting and hugging them, no matter what I was told.

One good day, they looked all over for me. I did not show up for breakfast which was unusual. I liked breakfast. I liked all of Miss Hedwig's cooking; she was very good. There was plenty of food, always, unlike in the camp we had just left. This morning I did not hear them calling me and Spitz had not been with me. Sometimes he did take off all by himself.

So here I am checking on Mathilde, the mama cow who was supposed to have her baby soon. I was checking on her, everyday, since I was told. Well, there was a baby calf this morning. Mathilde had calved over night and was busy licking it clean. I had discovered them and promptly climbed over the barrier and was now hugging this little calf at the same time Mathilde was in the process of licking it clean and, naturally, me at the same time.

When I was finally discovered, I think Spitz found me, he showed up in front of Mathilde's stall, barking, leading the search party right to my love fest. The grown-ups promptly ruined it by hauling me out.

Don't know why, it seemed perfectly okay with Mathilde. Mama was not happy and stuck me into one of those aluminum buckets to get all that goop from Mathilde's tongue off me. It took mom several days to get it out of my hair.

The next dilemma for them, not for me, was when I got stuck in the chicken coop, which had a square hole in one side for the chickens to get in and out. The eggs were inside the nest, under the chickens. So one day, I heard the old Mrs. Niemann say that she wanted eggs for breakfast. I thought, good, I will get them and took off. This time Spitz was on my side. The door to the chicken coop was closed so I crawled through the hole to get inside. Spitz behind me. He kind of scared the chickens which took off in a hurry, out of the hole, into the yard.

I proceeded to check the nest. Since I had no container, I gathered up all the eggs, I found, in my apron. Every girl had an apron. Then I got back to the square hole to find out I no longer fit through it, not with all the eggs in my apron.

I sat down next to the square hole and sent Spitz out onto the chickens. He liked that game. They made quite a racket, which attracted the adults, in short order. He was chasing them around the yard. It could have been a "fox in the hen house," but it was only little old me, gathering the eggs for breakfast.

I don't seem to have gotten into trouble for it. They were farmers, things happened on a farm, especially with children around. The old Mrs. Niemann, also known as grandma Niemann, showed up as well, to check the ruckus. Surveying the situation, she just chuckled, then under her breath remarked this would be a good experience for Hedwig. Once her husband was back from the war, they were bound to have children. She hoped it would be soon, before she had to check out. Then she walked off with the direct order to round up the chickens and get the eggs. She was ready for breakfast. "So get on with it." She was a no nonsense kind of old lady and reminded me of my own grandmother a lot. I spent the next two years practically in heaven (the farm) until we got two rooms in the village Epe, together with my grandparents.

Chapter 6

Dumping the Payload

"Bernhard," Hubert's nephew, had been 12 years old and remembers the following story from the war. It was 1942 when he was ripped out of a sound sleep in the middle of the night, hearing an ear splintering noise. He was living across from the train station on the Bahnhof Strasse. His dad was home for a short leave; he was a soldier. They ran downstairs and saw a burning airplane, a big one, a bomber. The noise was overwhelming. It circled overhead, on fire, losing oil and gasoline which had also caught fire. The oil and the gasoline ignited on the way down, leaving a fiery streak in the air. Bernard thought it would hit the tall chimney of the factory, just ahead on the right side. The chimney was 70 meters high and the airplane was heading straight for it.

Then the airplane opened its bowels and an entire payload of bombs dropped out down onto the factory. They were fire bombs and exploded near the chimney into the building of the *"Faerberei"* (a dye-shop) and a *"Schlichterei"* which is a sizing plant. The fire was immense and lapped over to the next building, igniting another fire. All around where the plane had dropped its payload of bombs, there was destruction, flames and fires.

Bernard and his dad stood there watching in horror as the burning airplane lost more and more height. The door of the airplane was open; he heard panicked voices yelling to each other. He could hear them clearly, it was in English. He did not understand it. But he knew it was in English. Shortly thereafter, the plane crashed between the bridge and farmer Johann Plietker's place. On its final way down, it took out farmer Plietker's barn and part of the house. It was still spilling gasoline and oil all the way down, which ignited the barn. The crew of the airplane jumped out very close to the final impact, but did not survive. Four dead soldiers lay around a crashed plane with one of them inside burned. One was a family man. His papers showed he had four children in England. The only one left in the airplane wreck was burned.

The fire department had to come from the next town over because the one in Epe had a "Panne," some kind of breakdown. The fire department crew came from Ochtrup. They came running down the train tracks and went to work on saving the house and the barn, first.

"That was not the end of my experience," Bernhard said. "I have another I witnessed after my dad returned to his unit. We were woken up, again, this time at 6 am in the morning with a big bang. We got up (my mom, my sisters and my grandparents) and we went outside to check what had happened. Remember, we were living right across from the train station. We could hear loud and desperate cries from across the street at the station. It was a *heilloses durcheinander*, a total mess."

"There was no alarm given this time, so nobody knew what could have happened. No airplane had been spotted overhead," he continued relating. What had happened? "It was total chaos at the train station cries for help everywhere. Then we found out that a locomotive, with full speed, had collided with a working crew train on its way out of town. There were many people wounded but, thank God, no one dead." A track man had accidently thrown the *"gleis"* (track) to the wrong side. The signal man had made a mistake.

Mother and I had the incident on the farm where we stayed and had witnessed the bomb drop. The payload that had been dumped over the farm, while mother and I were living on that farm. It had killed a bunch of cows and the wounded ones had to be shot; they called it "emergency slaughtering."

By the end of 1944, four airplanes were shot down over Epe. One went down close to house Floebach, another one on the street Epe-Alstaette, behind the tax-house; the other two went down in Lasterfield, too close to farmer Schepper's house. Mutti and I were on the farm at that time. We, too, heard the sirens go off and, shortly after, we heard airplanes overhead and other airplanes chasing them.

The German aces, called *"Jaegers"* chased them and got four. The military came later to pick up the pieces; the area was cordoned off so nobody could take a souvenir, but I think they were worried about unexploded bombs.

Then it got really bad. It was at the end of the war but nobody knew it, really, because it seemed they all had gone mad, stark raving mad.

Now the fighters in the air came down; they were deep flying planes, and started to shoot at anything that moved, I was told. A child moving around, a dog, a wiggle in the grass, a guy on a bike. One could not tell at first sight if they were ours or were they the enemy so we were told, "dive under something, get flat on the ground, out of sight." We called these airplanes the *"Tiefflieger Angriffe,"* (dive bombing) attacks on civilians.

That was not supposed to be happening in Epe. We did get a little bit, not as much as the big cities. We were close to the Belgian soldier, or the English. They kind of flew over, thinking of a fast getaway. Only the German resistance in the places like Rheine and Muenster put up a bit of resistance, as big as they could manage. Not in Epe; we just sat and watched the sky, hoping for no more accidental payloads being released. The sirens still went off and we all scrambled into designated shelters.

This went on for some time. The last time I remember the siren glaring, we could hear the bomber up in the sky, wondering where it would drop its load today. Opa said "it's a B17." But it was not alone. A squadron of fighter planes surrounded the bomber.

Opa continued, "Where are our *Jaegers*; not one in sight?" Soon enough the bomber was sighted again on its return but the sound of it was lighter.

Now the neighbor Steinau, next door, remarked, "it's dumped the load, that's why there is a lighter sound!"

How they could tell, I don't know. Then we saw them, *"na endlich,* the *Jaeger,"* somebody called out. Finally they showed up. The German fighter planes were up in the air engaging the enemy and we watched the air fight, way up in the sky. The bomber, the mother ship, kept plowing through the night sky, but the squadron surrounding it broke formation and went engaging the *"Jaegers."* This was coming closer and closer and soon enough we heard explosions, some going down.

Then we saw the German fighter planes chase two of the fighters; they encircled each other and they were very low, too low.

Mr. Stenau remarked. "He is going to get stuck in the trees."

Opa, told Oma,"Get her into the house," meaning me, but Oma just put me behind her skirt. I still could see, I peeked around it.

Bang, the German pilot is going to crash. Sure enough, he came so low that he shaved off the top of trees, then went straight up into the sky, firing. When he pulled up, smoke came out of his engine and he fired up some more shots which hit the other 2 planes he was fighting. He hit them. They went down. They were so low, maybe 500 feet, and in desperation they jumped out with their parachutes which did not open; it was not high enough. They plunged to their deaths. Two planes full of men.

The German pilot went down, also; he had to, his plane was hit, as well. In a nearby meadow, he completed an emergency landing. Then he headed out to the crashed plane, his pistol drawn. We all did by that time, including me. "How come they took me, you want to know?" Well, where would I have been put at that age? It was close to the end of the war and we were going to move into an apartment which Oma called the chicken coop. It once was and then it was remodeled, a little bit. There were no baby-sitters, then.

We all went to see the site. The entire village came to look, just alone to find out was it one of ours that had crashed. They had seen both planes going down. Mother was to keep me way in the back. I still could see.

Dead pilots, all of them. They were strewn over a small area which now had been cordoned off by the police chief. The *"buergermeister"* (mayor) was here as well, palavering on what to do. The German pilot had collected all the identifications of the enemy flyers and placed them in a plastic envelope to take it to headquarters. His plane was done for and could not be flown out.

Hubert, the ranch hand from the farm, showed up right next to us. He hobbled over and stood next to mom; I think he liked her. Mom didn't; they were the same age, about 25, and he had no girlfriend, Oma had said. He had been close to the plane, last night, and heard the pilot say. "That is my 40th hit; I will get a ribbon, a medal, for it."

Then grandpa turned around and he spotted a group coming up from town. It was now 10 am in the morning.

"Who is that and what is that supposed to be?", Grandpa asked.

The old Mrs. Niemann had joined us up front and remarked, "that is Mr.Trumbel, the headmaster of the boys school. He is bringing his 8th grade class up to see the crash. I guess he is doing a field trip for his 8th graders. Who knows what he is up too, he is a pacifist."

Mr. Trumbel had arrived by then and formed a line around the crash site, pointing his students to take a good look.

"Crazy old goat," I heard my Oma say, clearly I heard her, standing next to her. "Why did he have to show this mess to the boys?"

Everybody got upset that he had brought his class here. Then grandpa gave his two cents which he seldom did.

"This might dampen the enthusiasm for a hero-worship. Once you see the carnage up close and personal, you look at war with different eyes!"

Mr. Trumbel had been on a mission, so to speak, all here at the crash site knew it, well maybe not all, I surely did not know what was meant. I just wanted to see the planes.

Chapter 7

Did We Get Bombed Or What?

"Did you hear that, what was it? I thought the war was not over here, not in this small forgotten town, this hick town," mom said. "We are out in the boonies, on a farm. Nowhere near a big city, or anything important. They promised us." But what does that mean, they promised a lot of stuff, nothing materialized.

"Who are they?", I wanted to know.

But she ignored me and I forgot about the question, soon enough; I was too little.

It was the middle of the night, mother was upset, something woke us up and she started to get dressed in the dark. I wondered what is going on. I could hear noises downstairs in the house. I can hear Grandma Niemann giving orders, the young Miss Hedwig is crying; I can hear it. I wonder why? I wanted to get out of the bed, I share with mother and go down to look. But mom is just listening at the door to find out if she could overhear what is going on downstairs. Now we can hear the voices of the field hands; they had come in from their bunks across the way, over the hayloft. They are in the kitchen and they are talking nervously.

Finally mom is getting up the courage to go downstairs to find out what has happened. What was this thunder that had roared over us, with streak of light, as if on fire? I am right behind mom, not dressed, just in my nightgown. We had wood floors upstairs in the bedrooms and cement floors downstairs. As soon as my bare feet hit the cement flooring, I wished I had looked for my shoes. It was very cold and I climbed onto the wood breakfast bench, to listen. Nobody told me to go back to bed. The farm hand, Hubert, was the one with the funny leg that had prevented him from being drafted into the war because he dragged it behind him. They called it a Clubfoot, he said.

"It's a bomb, or a payload that came down. We had that happen before. No reason to get upset. We are so far out of town, it must have been a *"Fehlanschlag,"* a failed hit.

"What do you mean, no reason to be upset, are you joking," snapped the old Mrs. Niemann at him.

"It's like the one in 1943," said Michael, the really old field hand with a very solemn face. "Remember, when we had that munitions train parked in the train station. Boy, we could not get it out of town, fast enough. If it had exploded in town, the town would have been gone, just blown off the map. We all were scared senseless. Then it blew up, soon after it left Epe, a bit further on its way to Bruendermann, over Gronau to Muenster."

Nobody knew if it was by accident or if it was hit by bombers letting go of their payload because they were chased by the German fighter planes. "This sounded like last time they had heard these awful noises, detonation, flames and smoke," Michael continued.

"Oh hush, will you," said the old Mrs. Niemann, "no need to bring that story up again."

"But something has come down. Last time it took out a soldier just home for a short leave," the old farm hand, Michael, would not stop, and he continued on. "That was one of my neighbors. Another time, the payload hit a house and killed two little girls inside." So they went on guessing what could be the cause of all this thunderous noise.

We were too far away from the next farmer; if they wanted to find out, they had to investigate themselves. Nobody wanted to go out in the dark and my feet were starting to feel like icicles. All were standing in the front now looking out of the kitchen window. One could see that something was burning in the distance. The war was still raging on, even here, in Epe where we were too small and too unimportant for action. Not really!

So far, we had a few hits close to the train station. We all knew; don't live too close to the train stations. You get hit by sheer accident. But we were all the way out of town. It took horse and buggy or a bicycle to get into town. Nobody had a car; well, almost nobody. I heard them discuss that train station again, whatever had happened out there. It was known the train station was important; it transported munitions, tanks, supplies and soldiers.

If necessary, the bomber would let their deadly load drop; they had to when they were trying to flee from the German fighter planes that went after them. Is that what we heard; did they lose the bombs right here on the farm, in the meadows, where our cows were? I could hear the cows; it did not sound like mooing, more like screaming, that is what it sounded like. I hoped it was not Matilda, my favored cow.

"Go check it out,"

I demanded of the men standing around looking scared. Nobody wanted to go check it out. It was dark, the middle of the night and they were not sure that it was over, whatever it was in the first place.

By the first light, the men armed themselves with pitchforks, with sticks, like baseballs bats. They were now ready to go check it out. The old Mrs. Niemann got out a rifle, a Mauser. It looked old, but she remarked it would do the job if it had to. She looked like she was dead serious. I knew she meant every word. While she went digging for shells, mother finally took me upstairs to get me dressed. Thank goodness, socks on my feet. The socks were knitted by Oma, who knew how to knit socks and gloves with fingers. Then I could hear a commotion in front of the house.

We raced downstairs. As soon as we got to the door, "guess what?" Grandpa and grandma showed up from the neighbor's farm. They had heard and seen the fire. They were worried and come over as soon as it became light. Now we all marched off to the meadow.

When we got to the small hill, Micheal, the old farm hand, who was leading this little group, tumbled into a big hole, a crater with smoke coming out of it.

He yelled, "Get me out of here, quick, I landed on something slick, cold, I think it is a bomb. (*Lieber Himmel, mach schnell*) Good God, hurry, get me out before this thing goes off."

They had brought rope, because of the cows, and Opa and Hubert had pulled Michael out of the crater and he rolled over the wet dirt, just in case it was a fire bomb. They often ignited later. Michael told everybody, "Get back from the hole; it is a payload (not all bombs went off) and there are also some pieces of cows all over the place."

He turned to the old Mrs. Niemann,

"Give me the rifle I will kill the cows that are wounded. We can't leave them like this. We will come back later with help to carry the carcasses into the barn." Then his gaze fell on me, just as if he had only realized then that I was here at all and shouted;

"*Bring das Maedchen weg von hier*, (get that little girls out of here)!"

"*Nein*" (No) I cried out, "Not before I see my cow!"

Then I saw that Spitz had already found her, among a small group of cows a little further away, under the trees, cowering together, scared and mooing pitifully. Spitz was over there, barking his head off.

"Hubert," ordered Michael, "Get the rope out of that hole and the rest of the cows out of here as well."

"Miss Hedwig, Herr Floreck," he addressed my Opa, "Can you help, as well?"

Then he and the old Mrs. Nieman went off to find and deal with the wounded cows. Soon enough we heard a bunch of shots, six to be exact, I heard Oma count them. What a shame, she said I saw a bunch of young calves before we were asked to leave.

Some of them had been killed by the bombs and the detonation itself; others had limbs torn off, holes in them, wounded horribly. The old Mrs. Nieman came back and reported hat it had been taken care off. Now we would wait for help to arrive, the meat butchered into the form where everybody could eat it. The butcher would arrive soon as word could be sent to him. He would come with his apprentice and go about his business which was butchering and making sausages, etc. There was a lot of work to be done.

Chapter 8

Someone Shot at Grandfather in Igel-Mosel

They came for grandfather, but he had been warned and had already left the house. The house was empty, the light left on, per instruction, to imply that it was occupied. They shot up the house thinking he was in it. He was not. He was not the only one in the house. Grandma was, too, and so was Anna, my future mother.

"Who were they?" I asked years later when I went back to investigate, still finding people around from that time. "Well, they were the police," then folded into the Nazi Party, controlled by them. Private citizens had been disarmed, nobody else had a gun. The guns had been outlawed.

So if they wanted to keep their job, if they wanted to stay alive, they did what was expected of them. Not all people agreed with that action but what could they do without getting in trouble, themselves?

So they called Ernst, now a Detective of Police in Cologne, to give him a heads up. His police buddies in Igel related to him that something was in the "Making" to warn his dad, a strike was planned.

The house was shot up that night, but nobody was in it. Then the news of this wild shootout went all over town and sensibilities went in all kinds of different directions. Grandfather was still working as a  custom officer and had years left on his career. He was very openly against Hitler. He was not the only one, but he was the one that could not keep his mouth shut. It went so far, in some cases, that children reported on their parents and got them in trouble.

Grandpa could never keep his politics to himself and this got him nearly killed. To make matters worse, his voting papers were marked, opened, so it was official that he was an enemy of the State, the Nazi Party. It had consequences. Soon he got the official letter, he was to lose his job, forced into early retirement, with fewer benefits than he would have with regular retirement. Now it was too dangerous to stay in Igel, this town, where everybody knew every body's business.

It was decided to move to Cologne, where two of his sons had already moved. Karl, was a master tailor; the other one, Ernst, a police detective. Then there was Willie, a master mechanic in Osnabrueck working for a large copper concern. The fourth son, Hermann, was floating around God knows where. He was in the Marines. I think this was either in or around the time he volunteered for the war in Spain. That is a different story. Then there was Anna who was about 17 years of age. She grew up in Igel. All her friends were there which she never saw again until I took her years later. Before they left, they buried all of their silver and other things in one of Uncle Karl's friends backyard. Much later, after the war, it was retrieved.

Had they stayed in Igel, they would not have been bombed out but they all deemed it no longer a safe place. Lots of people, after being reported, were taken into custody and sent to concentration camps. One did not have to be Jewish, although that would hasten the process considerably. Most of the people did not know this or they just could not believe it. If they suspected, they did not dare to mention it. Then, of course, there were those Germans that were OK with it, lots of them, who took advantage in any way possible. Nobody ever knew any of them.

Chapter 9

The War is Over and Now What?

It was Easter Monday 1945 when people in Epe left their air raid shelters and watched the advance teams, the reconnaissance vehicles (recons) coming down the main street and flanked on each side by soldiers. The people were standing on the sidewalk, or behind trees, watching as the winning forces marched into Epe. The war was over. In the days that followed, the village people returned to their houses from wherever they had been hiding. On May 8, 1945, WW II officially was announced over.

Now started the phase of humiliations heaved onto the German folks. The Nazi's were arrested, as well as Josef Schakelburger, Hubert's uncle who could not understand nor wrap his mind around how he could have been so wrong, having put his money on the wrong horse namely Hitler.

Thereafter, they collected all the women belonging to the official Nazi parties, marched them into the only movie theater in Epe and forced them to watch "*KZ Lager*" films. "What is *KZ*, you may ask?" They are Nazi concentration camps. The movies depicted all the wrong doings of the Germans. Later, everybody had to view these films to get re-educated and to make known what was done.

It was the Thursday before Easter when Fraulein Huber, who had worked in Muenster, tried to get home to her parents in Epe. She could not use the train; it was too dangerous and many tracks had been destroyed. She hitched a ride after having negotiated the fare with cigarettes. She had saved them knowing they would come in handy someday. Now she could bargain with them. Fraulein Huber managed to get a ride in an army supply transport, whose driver was a heavy smoker. He took a chance and so did she. If she would have been detected in her hideout under the tent that covered up the transport of the munitions cache, no telling what the consequences would have been.

Everybody suspected that the war was over but nobody knew for sure. She made it through several German road patrols on her way to Gronau, where he dropped her off, right next to the Lutheran church from where she walked four miles all the way home to Epe. Gronau had been destroyed as well; it was bigger then Epe but not by much.

Near her family's home, she came upon a troop of German soldiers who had barricaded themselves between her house and the Dinkel River and was led by *"Feldwebel Obermeier,"* the Sergeant in Charge, part of pockets of armed resistance still all over Germany. He was going to hold his position right here with the Dinkel River as his line. Fraulein Huber just arrived from a totally destroyed Muenster with information that the war was lost and there had been a surrender. She was not believed. In painful realization, Fraulein Huber continued to persuade the small groups of soldiers to stop fighting, that the war was lost because of what she had seen and heard. It had not reached all corners of Germany yet. She told the Commanding Sergeant to stop this *"Unsinn"* nonsense and to give up his stand here. She could have used different words but she was tired, frustrated and where she had come from the news had spoken of an unconditional surrender. She was through mincing words; all she wanted was that it would be finally over.

There was resistance here and there, stubbornly, or maybe fearfully clinging to the mantra *"we will not lose,"* the Fuehrer told us. The soldiers looked very young to her, really just boys, not even old enough to have been drafted except for the "In Charge Sergeant." He was not going to give up. He had orders to offer resistance to all enemies of the German regime. He was barricaded and was going to shoot, if necessary.

He got very angry when she repeatedly told him to stop this *"Unsinn"* nonsense. Then he threatened that he had the military right for an *"standrechtliches erschiessen"* and he could shoot her. In war time the right to shoot anybody, not following command, being thought of as a deserter, a traitor or just plainly keeping the military from their job could result in *"standrechliches erschiessen."* Dead in whatever form it comes: you would still be dead. He had pointed his weapon at her.

Her mother was watching the front of the house and had just hung out a white bed sheet through the window. That did not calm this trooper down; it enraged him further. Everybody became extremely worried and piled out of the house to prevent him from shooting her. After all, he could not kill all of them; not the entire family! There was a momentary standoff which gave her time to escape into the house.

A few days later, the entire troop was picked up by an advance team of the English forces marching into the region with their tanks. Then came the occupation and, in Epe's case, it was a Belgian Military administration. Agatha Strasse was cordoned off and the houses on both sides were confiscated for housing the military *"Besatzung"* (Occupation). Those were the big houses of the upper class; the storekeepers, the factory managers and the Stenau's, right next to us who had a coal business besides being farmers. We had to get to our house from the back side. Herr Gubermeyer had to give up his house but he had two so it did not matter that much to him.

The German counterpart having to deal with the occupation forces was the Mayor. It was Herr Gubermeyer who also was Director of the local union. By nightfall, a curfew was applied and nobody was allowed on the street. If they caught you, they jailed you, no exceptions. Nothing was to be tolerated. Some people wrote on their fences, *"here live eight Catholic people,"* which did not help. No church services were allowed after dark. Neither did it help the most beautiful girl in Epe Johanne Kamper. She was caught sneaking out to see her boyfriend and ended up in jail much to the embarrassment of her parents.

Now the war of survival started in earnest. All businesses were closed down, the factory was closed and no one knew if, or when, all could be opened up again. There was an attitude about to keep the German industries from becoming mighty again. It was to be agriculture only.

The small rations were shortened some more. Instead of wheat flour, we got corn flour and made it into yellow bread; it tasted awful. Here is also where the story with the *"Muckefuck"* started for us. The imitation coffee called *"Ersatz Kaffee,"* could be traced back before WW I and even into the war between Germany and France in the late 1800's.

In Epe, somebody by the name of Leo Niehoff on the Schiller Strasse had a small grocery store and he started roasting all kinds of beans, corn, buckwheat, acorn, etc., to get as close to coffee as possible. The Niehoff grocery store is still in operation, now in the 4th generation of owners.

There was imitation coffee, imitation bread and there was no sugar at all. When the first sacks of sugar arrived, it was in brown burlap sacks and the sugar itself was also brown. I remember the marketing slogan when they advertised this *"Muckefuck"* under the name *"Lindes ja der schmeckt"* Lindes; oh, how good it tastes!

50

Another problem were all the foreign workers, the ones from Poland and Russia that the German previous *"inhaftiert"* held as prisoners and used as forced laborers. Now they were free and loitered around, stealing and intimidating the folks. But the soldiers, the occupation troops, did as well. The soldiers would show up at your doorstep with their girlfriends in tow, search the rooms, demand food, clothes and shoes. If they happened to come across a size that fit them, they took them right off the person that had them on.

Terrible love stories floated around. Then there was this rush of people dying or committing suicide for no good reason that we were able to see. There was Lieselotte, next door from us, on the Ochtruper Strasse. She tried to commit suicide when her fiancée left her standing at the altar, literally. He had taken up with another women in Muenster and neglected to tell her. He was a coward. He just let the day of the wedding arrive and then did not show up with no word at all. She had been crying for a week. She could not get ahold of herself and was finally found having taken a bunch of sleeping pills, but not enough. They pumped out her stomach and Pastor Heinrich's job was now to guide her back into his flock.

Then there was the shoemaker! That was a surprise! He is the one that was supposed to sole my shoes. I had worn them down and now it made me walk funny. There was a sign on his one room business.

It said: *Tut uns leid, Manfred Hesselman is tod.*
Messe am nexten Samstag in der Agate Kirche 10 Uhr.
Translation:
We are sorry, Manfred Hesselman is dead, Mass next Saturday
10 am.

The smell in his store was bad. It smelled like rubber, of course; he soled the shoes with it. Up front was his business and equipment to repair shoes, his bed and a sink plus a two burner plate right behind the curtain he drew across the room separating the two areas. I thought he died of that awful smell attached to the shoe repair. It kind of made you sick if you hung out in his room too long. He was a "*Mensch*," used when one wanted to convey that somebody was a good human being. We, Opa, thinks he killed himself but there was no autopsy; they just took him away. It had been rumored that he accidentally killed himself when cleaning his gun. "Wait a minute, his gun. Where did he get that gun and what kind was it?" It was a Luger issued to Army Officers, military police, airmen and tank operators in WW I. It was not turned in by him. All the guns were confiscated by the occupation forces a while back so what was he doing with a gun? It was an antique gun from WW I. It must have had meaning to him. "Just the same, what in the devil was he keeping it around for?" Opa thundered for a few days. "After all, he was right next door to us?"

That made Opa wonder if the old Grandma Niemann, from the farm, turned in her rifle? We did not think she did. Back to Manfred and that nobody believed the accident story. The Pastor insisted on the "accidental death" so that they could bury him in the Catholic cemetery. I heard Oma and Ope discuss it; it seemed like he was waiting for his wife to came to Epe from Bielefeld but she never arrived. He got tired of waiting for her.

Then there was the young Dr. Henninger just back from being a prisoner of war. He was not yet back a full year and he could not assimilate back into German society so he killed himself. He was successful about it. After all, he was a doctor and knew how to do it. He took poison. "What was it he no longer was able to live with? What did he see or what had he been involved in that he could no longer live with?" They say his brain was damaged; he was ruined and he could not go on. There was no wife. He himself was not originally from Epe but he moved up here. He made himself go in an easy way, Oma said. We never found out "*why*," what was it that troubled him in such a fashion that he no longer could tolerate life, now that the war was over.

Then there was Fraulein Joedel, a school teacher, who tumbled down her flight of stairs and broke her neck. She was very heavy and we think she lost her balance. She is the one that did a lot of spanking in the first grade. She had her balance then: she would climb behind us to hit us. I was not sorry when I found out. She was mean; we called her " Hexe," the witch. The entire school had to go to her funeral but we were not allowed to see her in her coffin. I would have liked to see her, but I did not tell anybody, because that would have made them think I was unkind. Well, in her case, I was definitely unkind.

So this was what it was like after the war ended. All of us suffered. No one was left unmarked. We all paid a price, for war is a tragedy.

Chapter 10

Muckefuck

Did I get your attention? I bet I did! Now you think I am going to swear, don't you? I will not. Believe it or not, I remember *"Muckefuck"* as coffee. Not good coffee, but coffee nonetheless. It has been on my mind lately, don't know exactly why. I thought about it for a while, then I went to investigate. A long forgotten drink brought back into our lives, right in and after the war; bitter tasting, a lukewarm cup of something called *"Muckefuck."*

Grandma complained about not having her "real coffee." I thought she would have done a great deal to get her hands on real coffee, she said so. I think she might have been seriously considering any option like going barefoot and naked through the snow if it had done any good. Nobody had real coffee. At least nobody we knew.

"Muckefuck" was a coffee-like drink made out of grain. It was a substitute or imitation drink; *"Ersatz Kaffee"* or *"Muckefuck"* same thing. There were lots of *"Ersatz"* items all over the place. There was substitute bread made with potato

starch, called war-bread. I also remember, we all went onto the fields after harvest to collect the left over that had been spilled (grains, corn, buckwheat, acorn and so on). We ground them through the coffee grinder and used it to make something.

In Epe, there was a grocer (Le-Ni Coffee substitute) that actually had a coffee roasting place and produced *"Muckefuck,"* right next to where I lived. His name was Leo Niehoff, and several generations later it's still operating. The names of this coffee changes in different areas of Germany. In Epe, they had a Dinkel coffee! It was named after this little river called Dinkel that ran through town.

In the 1870, "during the war with the French, a version called *"Mocca faux"* (translation false coffee, extremely thin) is found in the books. Around the Rhine area, the name is picked apart as *"Mucken"* (for brown wood) and the word *"fuck"* (faul in German) meaning exactly the same thing in English, foul, just spelled and pronounced different." When grain is used to produce this coffee, the word

"Muckefuck" is widely used. Now it is used again as a by-product to give the coffee color and more bitterness. The food industry has taken an interest again, using it as ballast ingredient.

Everything was rationed! Without official papers stating how much you should get, nothing happened. Eggs, fat, milk, grain and most of the food items had a measurement like maybe "20g", etc., attached to it. The amount of the ration was specified by gender, illness or, like in above case, a hardworking male, or a mother with a child or expecting a child. Everything was distributed on rationing cards unless you had connections. There were always ways to get around restrictions then, like now.

Everything was rationed and older people remembered the winter of hunger, in WW I, named the *"steck rueben"* famine (root famine). All countries had the same situation. Russia and the eastern blocks limped along for many years longer than the Germans until nearly late 1984, most likely to the time that Russia officially gave up, at least so they say now. The Germans were pretty soon involved in what we all called *"Das Deutsche Wirtschaftswunder,"* or the German Economic Boom. I came of age in that time and would have been able to quit a job today and have 50 better offers the next day. I decided to come to America instead.

Chapter 11

Refugees (Fluechtlinge) in Epe

The refugees are coming little by little, until more then 1,500 came together in Epe and nobody knew what to do with them, where to house them; after all, they were not Roman Catholics. The entire region around Epe called *"Das Muensterland"* of Nord Rhein Westfalen and had more or less one religion. The refugees were Lutheran (Protestants) and did not fit in. However, the village was told by the new German state to find room and to integrate them.

The Catholic church had grounds outside the village way outside. A big piece of property overgrown with juniper, *"Heide"* (heather), a dirt desert so to speak. Around 1930, excavations unearthed quite a bit of potting and things going back to 4,000 years BC but then the diggings had stopped and it had been of no use ever since.

The church community came up with a plan to sell this land for *"10 pfennig"* (app 10cents) per square meter and have them build on it. So here was a complete settlement of refugees that eventually build miles away from the village, keeping all of them together and somewhat out of the village. That is where all the *"Fluechtlinge"* (refugees) would live. I remember they did not like the *"Fluechtlinge"* never mind they were Germans as well. They did get all the extra help because they had lost everything except the clothes on their bodies. The people bombed out had lost everything also, but it was the

"Fluechtlinge" that had the advantages. I never really understood why.

The village community with the refugees worked together and soon there was this new settlement they called *"Die Ruebezahl Siedlung"* after a mountain range in Schlesien where they came from. They were to take care of themselves, to feed themselves, to grow fruits and vegetables and have their own animals: pigs, chickens, goats and rabbits to take care of their own needs. They had their own school and churches and we, the children, were not to associate with them.

So, where exactly did they come from? There is a mountain range along the borders between the historical lands of Bohemia and Slesia. It is the subject of Czech folklore, as well as in Poland and the German Schlesien. The mountain region, the *Carpathian*, is the highest in middle Europe and riddled with the *"Ruebezahl"* (Bluebeard) legend. He is a capricious giant, gnome or mountain spirit. With good people, he was friendly. Sometimes he plays the role of a trickster in folk tales. His origin is out of pagan times. He is the fantastic Lord of the weather of the mountain. Unexpectedly or playfully, he sends lightning, thunder, fog, rain and snow from the mountain down below, even when the sun is shining.

One of the legends tells of him having kidnapped the King's daughter Emma and keeping her hostage in his subterranean realm. He gave her a *"Ruebe"* (plant root) which was magical and it could turn her into whatever form she wished. He wanted to quell her longing for her home. She finally agreed to become his wife; however, she did not mean it. She deceived him.

After a time, the *"Rueben"* started to waste away and she sent him off to get new ones. She wanted the correct count in his fields. If he could not come up with the correct count, he was to let her go. While he went counting, Emma used the remaining magic and turned the last *"Ruebe"* into a horse on which she escaped to her beloved Prince. Once reunited with her lover, she made fun of the mountain spirit and his love for her and called him *"Ruebezahl"* which literally meant, he who counts all the roots. She mocked him made fun of him by calling him *Ruebezahl*. It was very disrespectful. It made him angry and he took vengeance as an unpredictable weather spirit. He still roams around in the mountain range to this day and the stories about him go on and on. The settlement in Epe is know to this day as the *"Ruebezahl Siedlung."* I think the community gave it this name because they wanted the refugees to remember their old home far away.

Chapter 12

He's Got Lice, Mutti, I Can See Them

Who was this scruffy looking bum in *"Lumpen"* (rags) sitting on the rock in front of the small cemetery? Opa, Mutti and I just went by him and he looked familiar, so Mutti mentioned. He reminded her of somebody. He looked downtrodden with torn clothes like, I said, in *"Lumpen."* He had a beard and his hair reached to his shoulders with his arms sticking out of his top suit. His hands were red and choppy and he looked so familiar.

We had passed him, Mutti, Opa and I, but Mutti just had to go back and look at him again to make sure she was not mistaken. It just could not be, could it? This could not be her missing brother, the one serving with *Rommel* in North Africa. The one missing for months, believed to be dead.

"Ach Du lieber, oh my God!," Mutti exclaimed as she and Opa passed him. He lifted his head looking at Mutti and then his eyes passed her to where his father stood; he called out "Dad, it's me, Willie, your

son. Don't you recognize me?" Tears dribbled from his face leaving a path down his dirty face.

We all had come back closer now and Mutti could not believe what she saw. She had by now recognized his voice. This was Willie, her brother. This scruffy, full of lice and dirt, filthy young man was her brother Willie and they had just passed him and Opa had not recognized his own son. All the inquiries to the War Office had come back unresponsive; nobody knew what happened to him.

He told us when it was announced that the war was over, he and his buddies just took off the uniform, left their guns behind and took off for home. They somehow got civilian clothes in which they could not be recognized as German soldiers and went on their way by foot, by boat, by whatever means they could find.

It had taken them months trudging across parts of North Africa, Spain, France and then into Germany. Hidden from Allied Forces they might encounter, staying unnoticed, surviving by stealing food, eating garbage, sneaking onto the ferry between the continents, half-starved by the time they got to Germany, where they separated, each of them to find their families.

Opa, Mutti and I stood in front of him and they shook hands, a German custom, while Willie told his story of survival and I wondered if Mutti would give him a hug, but maybe not on account of the way he looked and smelled. He needed a good scrubbing down, for sure.

While I was trying to make up my mind about what was expected of me in this situation, I voiced my opinion by pointing out again the very obvious.

"Mutti, der hat ja Laeuse!" Mommy, he's got lice; I can see them. Are you going to fix him?"

It was 1946 and the war was over.

Chapter 13

A Hectic Year

It's been a hectic year. It seems that I was tumbling from one strange situation into another over this year. Sometime in 4th grade we moved from the remodeled chicken coop into a real apartment on the Bernard Strasse, 3rd floor, over a carpenter shop right across  the Lutheran Church. The entire 2nd floor was occupied by Dr. Nuenning's family. We finally had a toilet (no bathroom) inside our place which made me extremely happy.

The housing we moved from had only an outside "plump klo," known also as an outhouse. We had a living room downstairs and behind that was a room that opted as kitchen, plus a bedroom for my mother with a trap door into a "Keller" (basement) where you would not go without a baseball bat because it had rats. My grandparents had a room in the attic, way upstairs. We had to walk through the corridor, up two sets of stairs, in the dark or with a candles to get to that room. There was no indoor toilet in this house.

I slept with them in that room. If I did not take care of my potty business before bedtime, I was sheer out of luck. In winter, one would freeze to death, catch a cold or something; besides there were rats outside. I could not go alone anyway at night for various reasons not at least there was a chance I could slip and fall into the hole. Folks would lose all kinds of thing dropped into it by accident, especially if they came home *"blau"* (tipsy), so I heard.

Items could not be retrieved, once they dropped down into that mess. This was not just an outhouse. It had a big hole underneath which was used as fertilizer. It was country farmland out away from big cities. Families had been ordered to be taken in until rooms became available and one had to manage! We had a roof over our heads at least, food and we were together. This had been a step up from the farm we lived on with the farmer and all the animals. I, however, missed Spitz and went to visit whenever I could.

Back to the bedroom up in the attic, with grandma and grandpa. We kept a chamber pot up there for me in case I could not last until

morning. Well, one night I didn't last and was groping around in the dark, half asleep to find the chamber pot. I missed! Next morning I found out that I had peed into grandma's shopping bag which was made out of cardboard material and did not take well to getting wet.

As to the rats, mom saw one peeking into the kitchen/bedroom of hers, before grandpa nailed a mesh from the outside over the window. Mom noted the rat was as big as a small cat. The basement door was also nailed shut tight to prevent them from coming in that way.

I did not want to sleep down there with mom, no way! I was up in grandma's bed. Well, that was actually before the end of 3rd grade and before we moved. I just thought about it remembering grandma was not too happy about my ruining her grocery bag.

Now back to 4rd grade and my big trouble over not transferring grammar from the blackboard into my notebook correctly. I remember it well because there were these two old biddies, maiden teachers, instructing us in German grammar. They were sisters and they had to instruct 40 children in that classroom. That in itself must have been a looming task. I copied the words wrong. She checked my book and found me wanting and whipped the notebook around my ears. She held me back after class to correct it or stay until I did.

I was supposed to be home for lunch so I send my girlfriend to tell grandma that I got hit and that I was still in school. I was lucky she just slapped the notebook around my ears. She usually stalked around swinging a thin bamboo stick. Depending who was in her line of fire they would get the stick over their fingers. She did not mind at all and she was not the only one. They all seemed to be severe disciplinarians. I got it before when I was talking in class but had not told grandma. I guess I felt I deserved it.

Not much time went by when I could hear my grandma's voice floating across the school yard, yelling and carrying on. She climbed the stairs to my classroom where she spoke her mind loud and clear. Nobody was to keep me after school when it was lunchtime. Anybody could see that I needed to eat since I was as skinny as a rail. Furthermore, if anybody was to do any hitting, it would be her.

She also carried a large shopping bag, a brand spanking new one, I want to add here because I had ruined her old one. It contained a steaming crockpot holding my hot lunch which she had prepared and I did not show up for. She plopped in on top of my school bench.

She was a force to be reckoned with, I found out that day. My very own secret weapon. Grandma was 69 years old. She had survived Hitler, air raids, 5 kids (4 of them unruly boys) for which she had received a Metal of Honor from Hitler. She had gone hungry too often, lost all her things several times over and on and on she went. "This I heard for the first time." Grandma received a metal *"Das Mutter Verdienst Kreuz"* for having produced five live children for the *"Vaterland"* the Fatherland. I would ask her about this later, for sure.

After this incident, nobody held me back or tried to use a stick on me. I found out right then and there that my grandmother had my back. It was a pretty good feeling. I loved her dearly for it; also, I never told her. But she knew it; it was there between us.

The not so good news was when she took me to the eye doctor where I found out that I was not really stupid, just nearsighted that was probably passed on from my father as well as his blood type of Rh-negative; nobody in my family has it or knows of anyone that does. So the reason why I could not read from the blackboard was that I was nearsighted. What the heck did that mean?

To my horror, they fitted me with eyeglasses and they looked awful, absolutely awful. My friends made fun of me and called me *"Brillenschlange"* (much worse than four eyes) which, in turn, made me want to hurt them and sometimes I did. I was still somewhat of a tomboy with lots of *"Winkel Hacken,"* (diamond-shaped rips) in all my dresses because I still liked climbing trees. I hated the glasses and would not wear them unless absolutely necessary in school or at the movies. Nobody important would be seeing me with them. I was told that there was a device called contact lenses but I could not get them until I was grown.

Next thing up would be First Communion and I learned what I needed to learn, yet I could not come up with sins for my first confession. I needed to confess my sins and I could not think of any. "What was I supposed to confess, what was a sin, and did I have any?" My grandpa came to my rescue and he wasn't even a Catholic. He wrote up a whole bunch of sins for me, like I did some lying. "How would he know that?" Also that "I did not listen well," that I could agree to and that was true enough and a few more that I used for my first confession. "Were they really sins?", I wondered, probably not but it worked. I learned them by heart and one more problem solved in my short life. This year was something else.

Then I got in trouble in school again for speaking up too much, asking too many questions and, on this occasion, I was found out that I had gone to the movies again against the teacher's suggestion. Well, I told her my mom took me and we went to see a Tarzan movie. Good grief, it took a lot of convincing to get my mother to go with me. This was not her cup of tea. This time I got her to agree to go, and I would be able use her as my excuse on Monday morning. It did not work; it became a mess.

The teacher told me, "Your mother does not know what is good for you." After all, my mother was never seen in church on Sundays. *"Ach Du lieber,"* (Good Lord) not that again. This is not the first time this teacher made some slight remarks about my mother not going to Sunday Mass. I told my teacher, "My mom works very hard six days a week and Sunday is the only day she can sleep in." Then I reported back to grandma.

71

Grandma got very upset this time and called her a *"Saumensch."* "I am going to tell that *"Saumensch"* a thing or two." Opa got into the mix by telling her; "Don't use that word, it's not getting you anywhere." Oh well, here we go again, one more reason for grandma to get dressed up and show up in school to straighten out that particular teacher on the point of what not to mention in open class. My mother's church-going habits were off limits. Now what is a *"Saumensch?"* It could be man or female, and it was not good. A *"Sau"* is a female pig. A German expression used about somebody's behavior it means nothing in English, but plenty in German!

All of this did not put me up to win a popularity contest anytime soon with my teachers, that were especially strict and totally of the mindset that a child should be "seen but not heard" system.

Then there was that bathing suit incident last summer. That is a separate story. This year was not over yet and more troublesome stuff was still coming my way. So far it was a very disturbing year. "What would be next?"

Well, grandma tricked me into seeing Dr. Nuenning in his regular practice. I don't remember exactly what excuse she used but the end result was a Polio shot in my behind which made me sore for two weeks.

I did not favor shots of any kind and was pretty mad at her for that ruse. She knew I would not have come with her willingly. She would have had to drag me so she outsmarted me. Well, I got over it eventually.

Then came a very bad winter and I had to see Dr. Nuenning again. This time I made her promise, swear on the Bible, no shots! Dr. Nuenning diagnosed that I was anemic. Here we went with *"Lebertran"* (Cod Liver Oil) for my bones which tasted gross. It was made from whale blubber. I checked out a book to read about it.

Actually, Eva checked it out for me. That was my friend whose mother worked in a library.

Now the anemic situation had to be handled and grandma had a remedy for that as well. Grandma had a remedy for just about everything. "So what was it?"

Each morning after breakfast, she concocted the following to make more blood for me: one raw egg, a big scoop of honey, some lemon juice and a shot of brandy. I don't know if it made more blood for me; what I do know is that I went to school in a good mood, very warm inside and did not get sick that winter.

Chapter 14

I Want To Read

"Fraulein Wiedemeyer, can I take that book home?" "Of course not, you know the rules no books out of the assigned classroom." She always raised her eyebrows, when she was annoyed. "How often will you ask me? You know the answer" and off she stalked. I was left wondering what happened to that courageous girl in the story. Did she become a saint or not?

Most of the books in that wooden cabinet were religious but I did not care; I just wanted to hear the end of the story. I contemplated how to get into the cabinet without getting caught. No matter how I turned this over in my mind, I could not think of a way. Again, she was slipping back into the classroom with raised eyebrows and in a highly annoyed voice asking, "Why are you still here? Go home! *"Kein herumlungern!"* Do not loiter around.

"Why was it so hard to get books?" There was a library in the village, with Catholic biblical and religious book that were all strictly morally deemed okay by the diocese. There were two different belief systems in this little farmer's village. Three-fourth were Roman Catholics, and the rest Lutheran-Protestant with whom we were not to associate. My mother went to the library often to check out books but never one for me. Her remark was always, "When you can read, I will rent one." It was only 5 cents and I could have looked at the pictures. They had some with pictures.

While she was selecting her book, I had skimmed the shelves and I had seen some children books, "Max and Moritz." How can I learn to read if nobody will give me a book? In school I had to wait my turn. We had 40 girls in class.

As for reading, I was not very good at it in 4th grade and I was almost 11 years old. I had no practice and no books to read. I don't know why grandma did not see to that. When it came to my time to read in class, I made sure I figured out when it was my turn and practiced my short little paragraph before they got to me. Nobody noticed except I knew it and I did not like it.

In Home Economics, the nuns read to us while we were learning to knit gloves with fingers, socks, dresses, aprons and pillowcases. When the story did not get finished by Friday, I asked to take the book home to finish reading it. The nuns would tell me; "Go and ask the room teacher," which always turned out to be Fraulein Wiedemeyer and I already knew how that would go.

I was told repeatedly not to asked so many questions. Grandma told me it's because we are not in the city anymore; it's farm country and people are very *"klein kariert,"* with not much imagination and not open to new or different things. They like their ways and we were dropped on them in war times. We had to learn to manage and fit in. "So, I was different then!" I am not sure I wanted to be "different."

One day on my way home from school, I met a new girl, Eva, who lived one street over from my house. She was different, I knew because people were talking about her and her mom living in one room. Nobody knew where they came from and there was no dad. No man in the house and people were speculating whether her mom had a husband or not. I guess they were dropped on Epe just as we were.

Eva was in the next grade up in the Protestant school. I liked her. She was always dressed up very nice and I could not see why she was different just because she was a Protestant, whatever that entailed. Come to think about it, grandpa was also a Protestant and I surely could not see anything wrong with him. Now that I was made aware of that I have to check into that, too.

Eva and I started to talk and I told her my dilemma which prompted her to declare. "No problem, my mother works in a library," the only private one the village had. "I can get you all kinds of books." "Oh my goodness, you really can, really?" But I don't have any money to pay." "Oh, don't worry about that," said this wonderful girl. "I will sneak them out and hand them to you through the window, you just have to make sure to give them back in proper time and not damaged!" "I will, I will I cried out."

This wonderful girl Eva supplied me with books of all types. Love stories, wild west, all kinds. When we ran out of one theme, there would be another. Then came the "racy" one. This was a private library and they had mostly novels, romance or other adult books. I read all I could get my hands on.

Some made my face turn hot and red, and I knew I had to hide them because I recognized the cover with a very skimpy dressed girl on it. It looked like the tobacco box that grandpa keeps his pipe tobacco in and that grandma would make snippy remarks about. He, Grandpa, sent me off to get his tobacco and always made sure I would take the empty pack so I would bring the right brand. I think he bought it because of that exotic girl on it with a flower in her hair. The pack said, "Jamaica Brand" on it.

However, as for myself, I was hooked on reading in the 4th grade. Nobody ever noticed me sneaking books in under my cardigan sweater and devouring them at a steady pace of three a week.

Now I wonder and I think grandmother knew, she must have, because she knew everything else and just plain thought it was okay that I found my own way to get what I needed.

Chapter 15

Kartoffel Ferien, Potato Vacation

It's October and we are out of school for two weeks. We are on what is known as *"Kartoffel Ferien."* It's fall and we are having a school break to pick potatoes. All the kids in school will; so will I, under great protest from my grandmother.

We were sorted into teams by the big boys. Those who would be strong enough to haul the potato buckets from the fields to the horse and wagon. There would usually be a line of 10 pickers, smaller kids. We picked in record time because nobody wanted to be dropped for being too slow. We had to keep up, filling the basket. The big boys, running in-between the lines, carried the basket and dumped them into the wagon on the road.

When it rained which was often at that time of year, we would be soaked to the bones, dirty, the wet earth stuck to the clothes, our hands and God knows where else. Grandma told me where. I don't want to tell you. It would be embarrassing.

I did not care nor did the others. The big boys had negotiated the daily pay which for the pickers was "3 *Deutschmark,*" or for short, "*DM.*" The exchange rate at that time was one Dollar to four "*DM.*" You figured out how much that would be now? The boys got a bit more because of the heavy lifting. My hands inside my gloves, (Oma's idea) were soaked and ice cold. The dirt was ground into my hands and nails.

At lunch time we were supplied with a big sandwich bag full of sandwiches and all kinds of lunch meat, homemade right here on the farm, apples and juice. They slaughtered their pigs and cows once a year, and a butcher would go from farm to farm to butcher all meat into delicious meat and sausages.

The bread was still warm when we got it. I liked it without the meat, just marmalade. Homemade bread, liverwurst and fruits. The apple juice was home made and it was so...... good. I would have come just for the apple juice alone, I think!

So much fun to be had. When we were done with the picking for the day, there was a big supper. This could only be put on by a German farmer. Among other things, huge pancakes with bacon pieces fried in them. Never ever have I tasted such pancakes again.

If I close my eyes and think real hard, I can conjure up that smell and maybe even the taste.

There were bonfires at night. The Fair was to be held just right after all the potatoes were out. The circus had came to town just in time for us to spend all this money we had made. By the end of each night, the horse and wagon would take all of us back into town and drop us off close to home.

When I got home each night Oma was waiting already in front to take off my clothes. She wisely, had provided very, old clothes for me to pick potatoes in. She complained that one could not get the dirt out of my wet clothes. The dirt did not come off from under my nails either, not for some time anyway. I soaked them until they looked like raisins. But who cared about that anyway, not while it came with such fun and excitement. Only Oma made a fuss.

She was trying to tell me I was a young lady now, almost, and should consider such things. "What things, dirty fingernails, really?" So in two weeks I made "30 DM" and it was all scheduled to be spent on the fair, on the bumper cars, the carrousel, the cotton candy, the Ferris wheel and the circus. I went through it in such speed that Grandma called me a *"Verschwender"* (spendthrift), whatever that was.

"I remember!" I had to pester grandfather to go onto the Ferris wheel with me. Neither Oma or mother would be going on. I was scared, too, but I wanted to go. Opa took me, not that it helped me much. I got so scared that when it started to swing up and around, I slid down his pants, hugged his legs and huddled there until the ride was over.

Well, so much for the wheel. But then there was the carrousel, the bumper cars, a contraption that was called *"Raupe"* or a caterpillar ride. Then one could shoot for teddy bears or other items. I wanted to try. However, grandpa would not let me. He said, "You are too small, don't waste your money." He told me he would not either.

81

His soldiering days were long gone, he had no practice. And then there was the circus. By that time I had run out of money but grandpa, grandma and mother went so I was given a break with the money. It was a good thing. I was broke.

Chapter 16

The Bathing Suit

I did not have one.

When summer came around I wanted to go swimming with the rest of my friends in the River Dinkel. It was a small river winding its way through our little village of Epe in the north of Germany, about 20 to 30 feet wide in some parts. In both directions it had several water holes where all the kids frolicked around whether they could swim or not. We sometimes found hidden treasures on the banks, objects left from the war. But swimming was our focus. *I am 11 years old, had no suit and could not swim!*

Last year grandma refused to buy a bathing suit for me hoping that would prevent me from joining the other kids, especially the boys. Girls and boys went to separate schools in separate buildings.

Well, it didn't prevent me from being interested in boys.

I was dying to find out about boys. Anything at all would do. Even just looking at them trying to decide which one I liked best. I had no brothers or sisters, nobody would tell me a thing. I was living in the dark, totally. What was that thing called love, anyway. What's that all about? How did it work? Well, there was a boy in church, an altar boy. I had a crush on him. I must have had since I went to church three times a week, before class, just to look at him. He had black hair and blue eyes. His name was Wolfgang Kubitzki. He was it, he was the bomb, the cat's meow. He was also a year older and had not looked at me once.

I hoped he would show up at the local water hole to swim. So this year I absolutely had to have a swimsuit and learn to swim. I just had to be around where he could see me. I just had to.

Summer had come, no suit yet. I had been highly motivated and in active negotiations with my grandma about a swimsuit. Grandma was definitely the person in charge. While my grandma was thinking it over, some of my girlfriends and I went off the beaten track to practice swimming. I figured my grandma would come around sooner or later and by that time I had already started to learn how to swim.

Not having a suit was a problem. I managed to tie my undergarment between my legs with a safety pin. I must have looked awful in my straight white undershirt, 11 years old, flat as a board and desperate to learn how to swim. A swimsuit could at least indicate, with ruffles, where my breasts would be one day. If I would be able to secure such a fine suit in the first place.

On both sides of the river were walking paths now empty of people because we were too far out. The only real entry into the river was through high grass. Getting in and out was a problem. Finally, I got tired of fighting my way in through high grass. I thought, why not just jump over it, right in, in the hope of landing in the river? So I jumped.

That what a mistake.

I came up short and landed in the grass and felt a dull pain in my heel. Something was wrong, I knew right away. I lifted my leg. Then I saw it. I had a gaping cut in my heel. *"Ach Du Lieber,"* (good Lord), will I be in trouble at home. They will find out I went swimming. That's all I could think about. I bent down to check when my hand touched something cold; I pulled it up. Holy Moly, I am going to faint, right here; I am getting sick. What I had in my hand was an army knife, a big blade. I called out to the girls. "Get me out of here, please." It was a bayonet, a side arm, left from World War II.

The girls helped me hobble out of the river. Just my luck we were observed by a young man having his lunch break at the river. He had been watching us. He came running, told me to get dressed and I did over my wet undergarment. He had run back to get his motor bike. He took control of the situation and instructed the girls, "Get her on the bike." Then he instructed me. "Hold on, I will drive you home.

This does not look good." He had tied a large bandana around my heel to hold the gap together. For some reason it did not bleed, I also felt no pain. That was strange. I am on the back of his bike with the blade wrapped up in the newspaper he had been reading.

We raced back into town to the doctor who lived on the first floor, in the same house. Then up to the hospital where Dr. Nuenning had to get rid of grandma first. She wanted to be in the OP, where he stitched up my heel but he would not have any of it, Mother told me. I remember they put a little cap on my nose and knocked me out with chloroform. I went out like a light, so I was told. When I woke up I felt awful. I wanted to throw up all day long. I had five stitches.

Grandma wasted no time to dispense some wisdom on her first visit. "Always look before you jump. If you jump into a pool, see if it has water in it, first!" Alright already, I had figured it out, while feeling sick to my stomach. The next day, the heel started to hurt plenty once the chloroform wore off. I had learned my lesson. I had also carefully studied my grandmother's face. Was she going to measure out punishment now that I had been found out? It did not look like it so I had been lucky!

I got out of the hospital after two weeks. There was a brand new bathing suit waiting for me at home. Grandma had instructed mother to see to it. We had no department stores in Epe. Mother cut out a picture of a suit from a magazine, got the material and took it to our seamstress. She made an obsolete fabulous suit for me, with ruffles.

Then grandfather was instructed to patrol the river at the swimming hole and to keep an eye on me. I would see him walking up and down with his friends, discussing politics and pretending not to see me.

I often wondered if anybody had thanked that young man whose name I never found out. I don't think I did. I can't remember. At times later, when I did, I would send up a little prayer for him, hoping he was happy, somewhere. However, when I got back to school, everybody knew what had happened to me and how I got my first bathing suit, and it was a grand one at that.

Chapter 17

The Spy Master

This still falls into the category of the hectic years, and it marks grandma as the ultimate spy master and me in training. It was not my idea so it had to be grandma's. I had no interest in mother's money but I had a great interest in mother's new boyfriend who wrote letters, love letters if you want to know the truth. I saw her folding them into a neat pile with a red ribbon tied around them, then they disappeared.

Mother finally got hired on in the Cotton Spinning Factory, the only employer in Epe. For generations they had provided work for this small village. She got the job due to grandpa's friend whose son was in a leading position. My grandparents, I mean grandma was going to let her keep all her money. She had to save it.

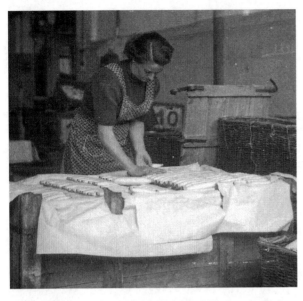

She did that at home, hiding it under the sheets and changing the spot every so often. But it did not matter because we, grandma and I, would go into a *"search action"* to find the new place, (always at times when mother was at work and grandpa was out with his buddies). Oma wanted to count the money, to make sure it was still there and check if it had increased each week.

I participated in this search to read the newly arrived letter, then folded it back carefully observing the correct way as not to get caught sneaking a peek. Love letters, of course I was interested in them. Oma's objective was to count the money because mother was known to lend money or be all around too gullible with her male friends. Mother never lost that tendency. Oma also did not trust the banks because of the devaluation of money she had gone through and the huge loss of savings. The money devalued so fast that if you bought a loaf of bread at 8 am for *"100 DM"* by 12 noon it was already at *"200 DM,"* or more.

I think this was also the time when Oma started to instill in me a pretty powerful distrust of the opposite sex. I suspected that grandma overdid her warning by a long shot. I believe that was her way to give me some pointers, the way she saw life. It had not worked with my mother so she started working on me, thinking that it would keep me away from men and not to be so trusting.

I was too young to care about that. However, she must have done a darn good job on me. It would show up later. I always had problems getting to trust men; actually not just men, all folks. I have been left wanting in that department. Where else could I have gotten that distrust if not from her?

She parted with another piece of advice in dealing with men. I remember it well. Number one: *"Never let a man hit you."* Number two: *"Make sure he is a civil servant because of the good pension."* Number three and this was most important; she told me, *"You must handle the money."* I acted on that advice, years later, and exchanged only the one about the civil servant. I substituted a new one, my own, number three was *"no ironing."* I can't remember what prompted me to add that one?

I called my grandma, Oma, and when asked who then is your mother, I would promptly say, *"Anna"* is my *"Mutti,"* which was mommy. It was perfectly clear to me.

I think at that time I had progressed from a grandchild to the position of confidante, or maybe even friend to my grandmother. I did not know it at that time but thinking about it now, it is the correct wording.

She never had any female friends; she had nobody to talk to. I was the only one bringing commotion into this hushed, damaged, but stuck in an old-world family. I would ask all kinds of questions and mother did not. It could have been that Oma just took control over me, away from mother and *"Mutti"* did not have the courage to take it back. All I know, she never tried either. I think, now, that it was so very convenient to not have to make all these decisions about raising a child.

Oma did not tolerate unfairness very well. If you had a good strong point and when I gave her one, she could see beyond herself. Mother would accuse her of hitting first and asking questions later. I did not see her that way. Well, it was sometimes! I see her as doing what was necessary at the time to get things done or move obstacles out of our ways.

As far as I was concerned, I could not have had a better grandma; she backed me through all kinds of situations, at school or with unruly boy companions. I was getting away with a lot. All the boys knew it, even the teachers.

I played more with boys because of the games I liked. We were on teams, we climbed all over the fences, antagonized the bulls on the fields and rushed back over the fences; hence came the holes in every dress getting caught on the fence. Then there were the potato picking excursion (not that many girls participated) and the ball games just to name a few.

I was allowed to save the green stamp which everybody got after we bought items. These were collected into "3 DM" books. I was saving for a bike. It took a long time. One day I took mother's bike to the bakery store down the street and forgot about it. I walked home and the next day, mother was totally beside herself because her bike was gone out of the shed.

That's when I remembered that I had taken it to the bakery store the night before had walked home and forgotten that I had used it. I rushed over there, before school, but it was not there any more. I felt pretty bad and deliberated on how best to fess up. I told Oma about it but she told me not to tell my mother, it would upset her even more. She would make sure that she would get another one. So my mother never found out that I was responsible for losing her bike.

Chapter 18

Grandfather Is Mad At Me

Never have I seen Opa that angry and, I don't remember what I did to get him that way. It's been on my mind. I have to ask mother.

I installed Yahoo voice on my computer and was calling my mother several times a week starting to ask about things, long past, hoping she would remember so I could record it.

"Mom, I have to ask you! What happened when Opa got mad at me and threw his shoe after me? Then chased me down the stairs and when he could not catch up, his shoe came sailing after me?" I was too quick. I got to the end of the steps around the corner towards the next set of stairs when I heard something slamming into the wall, right when I went around the corner.

"What was it that made him so mad? Mom, can you remember?" Mother laughs; I could just see her face. We were on the phone, again, on one of our weekly calls to each other.

"You don't remember at all?" she asked. "Nope," I said. "So what was it. Tell me. What did I do to anger him so that he found it necessary to chase me down the stairs and throw his shoe after me?"

"Think back!" Mother said, "He had a small bottle of schnapps next to his bed!" I think it was *"wacholder"* (white juniper-schnapps), a gin variety, of which he would take a sip each night or when he felt like it." "Yea, I remember that now that you mention it." It had just popped back into my mind.

Now I replied, "Do you mean he found out I would take a nip, sometimes, on my way to the toilet?" We had to cross their bedroom, grandma's and grandpa's, to get to it.

"Yes," she said. "Do you remember that you once fell out of bed right over him? Then they made you sleep in my bed in the kitchen?" "Really, I remember that they booted me out of their bed when I was 10 or 11. I thought it had a different reason. You know what I mean? I got too big to be sleeping in between grandma and grandpa!"

"That too," she said, "but there was more than one reason. You were a very restless sleeper. Sometimes you actually got up and walked around in your sleep so they had to get up, collect you and put you back to bed.

Mother continues. "One time they found you getting out of the living room window onto the roof, all in your sleep. This prompted grandpa to fasten a special lock on the window which rattled and woke them up before you could get out."

"Good grief, I was a sleepwalker?"

"Then they decided it was time for you to get out of their bed and into mine, in the kitchen, where I could hear the rattling on the window if you went sleep-walking again. Yes, as you guessed, you were getting extremely nosy. That was another point of their worry. Sleepwalking had started one night out of nowhere, then it stopped. Dr. Nuenning just told us to keep the windows and doors locked at night; that's all he could recommend."

"Mom, get back to the story of grandpa getting mad at me. What was it, tell me." She said, "I am getting to it, just hang on a minute." Mom started laughing and went on with the story.

"The point was that grandpa had accused me and grandma of sipping on his *Wacholder schnapps.*" The bottle did not last as long as he expected." Mother continued and said "I did not do it! Oma got mad at Opa and told him he should know better then to accuse her. She did not like hard liquor and he ought to know this after all the years of being married to her. So who was left? It had to be you!"

Mom said that Opa then sat out to trap the culprit by marking the bottle. He had been a custom officer and he knew how to get to the bottom of things. " Remember," mom goes off into another story, telling me that border story again. Opa had been checking people between the border of Germany and France for undeclared goods. He was a stickler for doing his job. Sometimes he overdid it. He literally became downright uptight about doing his job.

Mother said, "He once chased a women he suspected of smuggling something but couldn't find it on her. She had eggs hidden inside her garments, actually in her underwear. He followed her out of the booth and when she started running, he went after her and, soon enough, the eggs started falling out from under her skirt, one by one, until they were all out and broken. She than ran off over the border where he could not follow her."

"Mother, don't get off the subject. We were talking about Opa throwing a shoe after me. What of that story. Please, get back to it!"

"Okay, as I already said, he started to mark up the *schnapps* bottle and he watched you. He could not catch you red-handed and it frustrated him greatly. He added another trick by putting the *schnapps* bottle down, just so, measuring what spot it was in. Now he would be sure; if it had been moved, he would see it. Still he never saw you and soon he had enough of it and he was going to confront you."

"He told Oma and me that he was sure it had to be you but we could never detect any smell on you. He kept on replacing the bottle at a greater speed than he expected. Maybe it was done by the *"Heinzelmaenchen,"* a pack of fairies (gremlins), suspected of performing good and more often bad deeds in the middle of the night."

The *"Heinzelmaenchen"* story was used by people when they could not come up with a better one."Opa insisted it had to be you. He just was not able to catch you. It drove him nuts and grandma told him this was his mission and she was not going to help him. For whatever reason, she thought it was all poppycock."

Mom went on now but she got off the subject again by saying that grandma did not want to get grandpa angry with her in case she picked the wrong side. She remembered what happened when she stepped over the line and hurled a wet wash cloth at grandpa when he overstayed his card playing time with the boys. He came home very late and she was so angry that she lost it by hurling a wet wash cloth at him. Grandpa stopped in his track, looked at her and remarked; "It looks like I came home too early again!" Then he turned around and left, not to return for the entire night. Nobody found out what he did for that night, either. That cured grandma and she was more circumspect. Also, she was known as a "hit now and ask question later" kind of person.

"Oh, Mama.... get back to the previous story where grandpa hurled his shoe after me, please!" So mom continued, "He tried to confront you and you told him, nein, (no) you did not drink his *schnapps*. When he insisted you told him Can you prove it? That made him really mad and he called you, *eine verdampte Rotznase,* a damn brat. Whatever you said to him after that set him off and he went after you, promising you *Eine gute Tracht Pruegel,* a good spanking. God knows," mother said, " I don't know what he was attempting; he never ever put a hand an any of his kids. Maybe he was just trying to get you scared enough to leave his *schnapps* alone."

Question is, "Why did you sip his *schnapps?*" "Really, mom, all I remember is the shoe sailing after me. It's the only time I saw him angry and lose his cool, so to speak. I don't even remember why I took the sips; I did not like it and that's why I stopped. It was not that important to me. I don't really know why I did it, probably because it was there, and I could!"

Chapter 19

Who Is Guenter

Back from my first vacation. A tour to Cologne where we stood on the rubble of the house that we once lived in. I was dolled up, a beautiful dress with a big stiff petticoat which presented a problem sitting in the backseat of the VW, with Oma. I did not want my dress to be bent. I am 13 years now. Uncle Hermann had come to pick us up and I had been promised a visit to the zoo. What a glorious experience. The first time I saw real lions and tigers! On the way back, it was suggested we go to Osnabrueck and stay a week. Never before had I gotten such an invitation.

Little did I know for what reason we were taking this trip, out of the line of fire, away from Epe. When I found out, I did not like it, not one bit.

We got back to Epe and there I found out from mother a boy had arrived in Osnabrueck in the time we were gone. He was claiming to be Uncle Willie's son who had come from Igel by Trier to visit his grandparents. "Well, good luck with that!" We, grandma and I, had been sent away, out of the way, leaving grandpa to deal with the situation.

Guenter had come to see his grandma, maybe thinking she could help him establish some kind of connection to his father. I did not know that I had a cousin. Guenter had announced himself in a letter of which I had no knowledge. If I had known, I would not have gone with them on this trip. That is for sure. Mother told me she also was surprised when Guenter showed up. I was aghast, devastated, that I had missed him. I did not know anything about him. He was already 14 years old and had come by train, all by himself, to find nobody home. What a shame. What an absolute shame. How could this have happened? How could we have missed him?

Well, I soon found out it was not by accident. It took a while for me to grasp the story. Oma had left because she was told not to be around; hence they, the uncles, orchestrated this small getaway vacation. I should have known because Oma never went anywhere and left Opa alone "when he could not heat a pot of water." He was totally useless when it came to feeding himself, she said often. They took me as well, believing it best, since I had reached the inquisitive age of a teenager.

At that time, Uncle Willie was still married to Guenter's mother but was trying to divorce her. He had found Irmchen or she had found him, depending on whose story you believed, and he was living with her. Divorce took an awful long time in Germany especially if one partner did not agree. Guenter's mother, Lena, did not agree and it was dragged out for years.

The reason had been Uncle Willie's propensity for messing around then, now and still, whenever he could get a chance. They all knew it, and now I was to find out this messy story. Oma was loyal to her son and did not want to upset Irmchen. Uncle Willie had no interest in seeing or knowing his son. Actually, he never allowed Guenter to come and visit him. He always found a reason, being occupied at the time, so it never happened.

Only Opa was there and my mother. So Guenter just visited with grandpa and mother and then went back home. It took several rounds with mother, Opa and finally grandma for me to get to the bottom of it.

"So what was it?" Uncle Willie had left his wife, Lena, reason unknown, but most likely she left him because he was a womanizer. Thereafter, he did not want anything to do with her which included his son, Guenter. After the divorce became final, Uncle Willie had to pay Lena *25 Deutschmarks* a month. That went on for a long time. Lena stubbornly insisted that Uncle Willie had to pay what was due her.

Grandma and Uncle Willie's brothers, now all with new wives, stuck up for him, right or wrong, and his first wife and his son were no longer spoken of. A blanket of silence was placed over the entire situation. They would speak of it in hushed voices, and I had missed the connections until today when I came back and found out about the boy Guenter and his visit. My goodness, I had a cousin. I would be thrilled to meet him.

This was the first time I sat down with grandpa; actually, I made him sit with me to tell me why. He could not tell me "why" only that it happened. Yes, indeed, Guenter was one of his grandsons. Uncle Willie's son and he had come to visit, and found no one here to meet him.

Then I went to grandma. "This isn't right," I told her. "I don't understand, this is not fair, let alone the good manners you keep instructing me with. You keep telling me to be good and upright and so do the priest's in school. What is up with that? It this uprightness? "Is fairness only there for some people and not for others? Is it only when it suits you?" Grandma had no answer! I did not let them get off so quickly.

"What about my dad? He is still missing in the war, but Guenter's father is right here and he does not want to see him because he has a new woman. It does not make sense! Do people get divorced from their children?" I got quite enraged about it and went on. I called him "Drecksack," a dirt bag, but I think it is more closer to "bastard." "And you let him get away with it? How could you?" I blinked for a second having used a bad word, a grown-up word but nobody reprimanded me, least of all grandmother.

"I want to see Guenter, no matter what Uncle Willie has to say about it. I am going to write him. I am going to invite him to visit next summer. You better get used to that thought." I had tossed that sentence out and it was hanging in the air and left me wondering what kind of obstacles I had to overcome.

Grandpa looked at me and then turned away but not before I saw him grinning. I knew I had his approval. He was a man of few words. Often one would ask him questions and it took days for him to respond. He would answer, just in his time. It surprised me sometimes. I had forgotten what I had asked and then a day later he supplied the answer. That was his way.

Guenter came to visit the next summer. He stayed for 2 weeks and for a little while it seemed as if I had a brother. Then things happened, life happened. I did not see Guenter again until 35 years later in Igel. He had saved the postcard I had sent him all those years ago.

EPE i. WESTF.

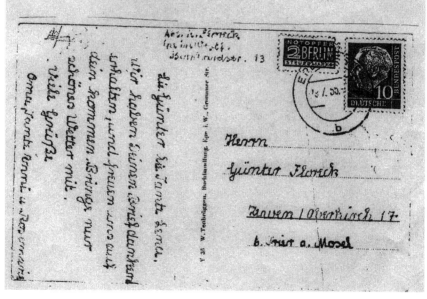

Chapter 20

The Boyfriend and the Moped

Udo Neil, rascal, boy scout, and maybe also boyfriend. He never declared himself, he just showed up on the periphery of my existence, the swimming hole on the river Dinkel. He was bombarding me with mud balls to get my attention. This was not his first maneuver to initiate contact; I was told by Rudy, my girlfriends older brother. Udo and he were on the same football team, actually it's called soccer here. He was getting tired of being pestered by Udo whose attempts had failed so far. I was formally put on notice that Udo liked me!

Well, bombarding me with mud balls was all together overdoing it. Why was he not just talking to me? Rudy said he tried, but I seemed too dense to get it. Rudy was sent to give it the direct approach to inform me, in case I needed to hear it, and that if Udo really had wanted to hit me the mud balls would not have missed.

I was surprised, here I had been focused on the alter boy, Wolfgang, all the while there was a perfectly good looking boy pining for my attention.

So started my first experience of having a boyfriend, he never asked me, or declared himself. We played ball and I was on his team. Never mind that we were not supposed to associate with the opposite sex. This was after school at the swimming hole away from the adults, nothing but meadows all around us and plenty room for ball games of any kind.

I spotted my grandfather patrolling along the river's edge again this year. We never acknowledged that we saw each other. At times, one of the other kids would yell. "Hey is that not your grandpa?" I would pretend to look and then shout back, "I don't know I can't tell from here!"

Thereafter we went to the movies on Sundays right after afternoon Mass. Actually, we arrived separate and made sure to stand in line behind each other. The tickets were marked with numbers. We knew that if we were standing behind each other in line, we could sit next to each other. We had to hurry to get there because the afternoon Mass ended just about the same time the movie started. I think it was by design. We were not supposed to go to the movies. Each Monday we did not escape the reprimand of the nuns and priest at school.

We communicated in secret by writing notes and they were delivered by Berny Nuenning, the youngest son of the doctor that lived in the same house. Berny was the *"Postillion d'Amour,"* delivering little notes *(Liebesbriefe)* back and forth. This went on for quite a while until Berny put the note under my doormat when he could not find me where my grandmother found it. She always found everything. I don't know how she figured it out. But she did.

There after, Udo, came up with a new strategy which was mirror writing. Once it was written a certain way it could only be deciphered by holding a mirror to read it. Still grandmother found my notes and now she was getting suspicious. She was wondering why I was getting notes with gobbledygook on it. I wondered how she managed to find my notes. She must have gone through my backpack. This was getting troublesome!

Again we had to improved our delivery system. He would deposit the note under the second bench in the nearby park, marked by a certain rock, and I would pick it up 30 minutes later. The next day I left the answer first and Udo would pick it up and so on. We did this all summer. I really don't remember what was so important in these notes. Was it that we were not to communicate or was it the secret of the process?

Then came this unfortunate Saturday at the end of summer, when Udo decided we should go the Holland on his mother's moped to buy stuff. He wanted socks of all things. Holland and the border between it and Germany was only about 2 or 3 miles from Epe/Westf; Holland also referred to as the Netherlands. There would be Customs Control and fees to pay. I knew this because my grandfather had worked as a Border Control Officer, after the Army. There was no fooling with these guys. They would hunt you down until they got their fee. People would go over for food but mostly they went to get cheap cigarettes.

Udo knew a way to Enschede a small border town without crossing Customs. That was the plan and entirely his idea. I did not need socks.

Candy maybe but not socks. However, I was fascinated by the prospect of the moped that Udo said we would use and he would teach me to drive. Here we were going through the back woods, the boondocks, the hinterland, on a dirt road. Water trenches (ditches) running alongside the very narrow road.

The moped was called a *"Maria's Hilf Motor"* or *"Brummfiets."* Basically, it was a bicycle with a motor hanging on the front handlebars, one had to pull to start, like a gas lawn mower. I think it was the forerunner of the motorized bike. It was very inexpensive and economical in gasoline. You could run on it for ever. It would not go very fast, but it was fast enough, which I found out soon enough.

We got the sock shopping business done and put the socks on our feet and in my case under my knee high. I was looking forward to operating the moped again. I pulled the string and when it started to crank up I jumped on quickly. Udo was already on the back seat. So there I went, happy, and not really that slow either. After all, I did well the time before and I thought it was a piece of cake. That was a great feeling. The wind in my hair, my pigtails flying up on each side of my head, and Udo hanging on to my hips.

Then I noticed he was yelling for me to slow down, *"nicht so schnell, langsamer,"* you are going too fast. I don't know how fast, but it was too fast for the curve that was coming up, which I did not see soon enough and all I could do is jump on the brakes. Well, I got it stopped with a thump. I did not crash but sort of leaned sideways and that is when I saw Udo catapulting over me straight into the ditch. I was surprised. I thought it was kind of funny. Udo did not think it was funny. He climbed out of the ditch, wet and scratched up, shook himself like a dog and called me *"Du Dumme Ganz"* Well really, Udo, was that necessary to call me a *"Dumb Goose."* Boy that was it. I never went out with him again.

I often thought about it later. I just could not forgive this *"Dumb Goose"* business. He was a nice boy and he never found out why I dumped him. He often intercepted my mom to inquire about me. I just could not get over that *"Dumb Goose"* business. I had no siblings was raised by adults, the only child, and nobody really communicated well in those days. I had no practice in fighting or arguing, I never needed to and it took me a lifetime of learning it.

So ended my first relationship.

Chapter 21

The Verdict

Halfway through Miss Herring's geography class, the door opened and Miss Wiedemeyer stepped in, surveyed the room, her eyes finally resting on me. Oh come on now! What did I do now? She proceeded towards Miss Herring with a newspaper in hand. She held it up for Miss Herring to see, then both buried their heads into it for a second. Then Miss Herring said, to me, "Rosemarie, you are excuse, please go with Miss Wiedemeyer."

Boy oh boy, what a morning this shaped up to be and I could not think of one single thing I was guilty of, not today, at least. I even went to church this morning before class. Miss Wiedemeyer swept out of class ahead of me and as soon as we were in the hallway she turned around and told me, "You need to go home."

"Why?" I asked, but she just shook her head and repeated, "Go home." I took off running.

If it was not me, it had to be somebody else in the family, an accident of some kind. She had not yelled at me, or acted irritated with me, which was her normal stance. After all, she was the head mistress of this high school and always looked irritated.

I was home within five minutes and scrambled up to the 3rd floor, falling through the door, where my grandparents were waiting. Grandma was sitting at the kitchen table with an open newspaper in front, white as the wall. Grandpa standing at the window, looking out, stone faced. A deadly silence surrounded them.

"What?" I called out, "What is happening, why am I here, right in the middle of school?" Grandma turned the top of the newspaper around, pointing to the front page, "Read!" she said.

There in bold letters on the front page, it said: **Death Penalty for Ernst Floreck, just in a few hours ago by a Court in Lyon, France, sending shock wave through the rest of Germany.** It further stated that the verdict had been reached in short order, in the matter of Ernst Floreck, accused of War Crimes. He had been incarcerated in Lyon for the last 15 years. Initially it was hoped that he would be freed, along with several other POW (prisoners), whose trials were still forthcoming. It was said that after 15 years of keeping political prisoners, France had still seen fit to put on a show trial and the need for a public spectacle. Protest had already poured in from around the world, especially from the German political order and other sources asking, and in some case demanding clemency.

"Good grief," what a circus this turned out to be after we realized that nobody would just willy-nilly put him up against the wall and shoot him, execute him. These things were not done any longer. They would have liked to, but after all this was Europe, not Russia, where thousands were still being held prisoners. They were just forgotten, conveniently forgotten.

The village put together several silent marches with candles. It was being reported in newspapers. Very important people spoke on his behalf. I never found out their names, they called, pledged their help and support. I know some of them were American Military. We received letters and boxes of goodies all the way from America.

A lot of attention was given to him and the rest of the prisoners. Facts, that no crime had been proved, did not matter; he belonged to the German occupation force in Lyon, France.

So the petitions dragged on and on for a long time. I found out just a smidgen of what it was all about. Was it true? I didn't know, I still do not. What did he do?

So what about Uncle Ernst, how did he wind up in this predicament? He was the academician, the smart one, the one driven to learn, to get an education. He went to college, supported himself by instructing students after his classes, to help with the cost. He wanted to become a doctor, but there was no money for it. He settled on joining the police force. He made it all the way to Detective when Hitler took over. All Police forces were absorbed into the Party, the National Socialistic Workers Party, shortened as Nazi party.

Uncle Ernst, being educated, was folded into the Weapon SS (Waffen SS), as an Officer, of the Military Branch. The other SS was in fact the Intelligence Services, and we all know about them, more then we really want to know. If he had not joined the party, he would have been dismissed, just like his dad my grandfather Karl, who was retired prematurely, because he was openly against Hitler, which got him nearly killed.  He could not keep his mouth shut. I think he passed that gene on to me, also his interest in politics.

Back to Uncle Ernst being in the Military SS, I wonder if that might be equal to the Military Police? He was not sent to the front but moved from one military prison, to another. Military Police are used there as guards. Reminds me of the TV show *Starlag 13* with Sergeant Schultz, however, I don't think it was that benign, ever. Then he was sent to Lyon, France, as occupation force, when the Germans invaded.

I personally believe he was smart enough to keep himself out of trouble, because nothing, no crime, was ever attached to him, but it did not matter; he belong to the outfit, the occupying forces. All that mattered was that he was around, even if he kept his nose out of the atrocities, which certainly had happened. When the war ended, he gave himself up to the American forces, which figured out where he was stationed last, then handed him over to the French Military.

He went to prison, was kept shackled hands and feet for two years. Out of many prisoners in that particular prison in Lyon, only a handful survived. There was a nightly raid and some prisoners were pulled out and executed. The others would sit in fear, each night, because it could be them. Uncle Ernst had his kidneys kicked in and damaged, which years later took him out.

After the first 2 years in prison it became better by and by, relations had settled down between Germany and France, but not by much. Uncle Ernst spoke French perfectly, which was a great surplus, because he could follow every detail, he made friends with his guards and often did paperwork for them, which made life a bit better for him.

Eventually his other brothers were able to visit him, they smuggled two journals out. What is in them? Again, I don't know. It was kept a secret. I think that he only detailed his treatment in prison, and that of others, rather then relating secrets from his military time. He would not have been stupid enough to write about that time, that would have been admitting he knew what was going on and did not stop it. That would have killed him for sure, even without a trial.

However, even relating the treatment in prison would have gotten him into trouble on both sides. The Germans would not want to confront the French by accusing them of maltreatment. The political system is the same all around the world, only in some places worse then others. It would not have helped in the effort to free him, or the other soldiers left in Lyon.

All of his immediate military bosses, the next higher commanders; managed to fly the coop. They all found their way to South America. They knew that no matter what they did, or did not do, they would have become prisoners, or worse. Most likely they would have been killed, just for their positions, alone.

Uncle Ernst figured, wrongly, that he had not done anything but follow orders, keeping his nose clean. It turned out to be the wrong decision, unlike his brother, Willie, who made his way back from Rommel's North Africa Army, by throwing away his gun and the German Uniform. Uncle Willie was just a soldier but he had sense enough to know how to survive. Uncle Ernst was forever attached to the war crimes, because he was in the SS.

Uncle Ernst was engaged to a woman in Vienna, who had given him a son. He set her free when it became obvious that there was no telling how long he would be kept in prison. She married somebody else and his son got adopted by her new husband.

When I finally met Uncle Ernst he was 45 years of age and mentally disheveled. He took a long time to reassemble himself, after spending 6 months in a government paid hospital, (Bad Pyrmond) where they flicked him back to health, or what ever health was left for him. He must have had friends and supporters in high place, because he had a job waiting for him with a German Co. by the name of Dynamite Nobel, in a high position.

He got married again and had one more son. Would you believe, when that boy went to school, other children went around calling him the Nazi's son? I bet those other boys parents might have been. Now, nobody had anything to do with the Nazis in the war. Uncle Ernst died at 70 years of age, kidney failure, compliment of his time in military prison.

"C est la vie" "That's life"

Chapter 22

An Act of Betrayal

Uncle Hermann, Grandmother and I are on our way to Epe in uncle's new Volkswagen, to visit grandfather's grave. He died the previous year, right before we all moved to the big city. Compared to Epe, this is a big city, with 120 thousand inhabitants. All of mother's brothers are living here now, helping each other to find new jobs and new wives. Osnabrueck was the city where they reassembled themselves and their shattered lives after this awful war and tried to start living. Only grandpa and one uncle, their brother still in France, had not made it.

I was 15 years old, had not seen my friends and missed them sorely. I had lived in Epe from age 4 to age 15. It was the worst time in a teenager's life to have been moved, transferred into a new system, left without any social contacts in the city. The new school did not start until fall.

After visiting the cemetery they took me, after much palaver on my part, to my friend Karola's house. What were they thinking, that I could be in Epe, not seeing one friend. God knows when I would get another chance. I was not having any of it. Both uncle and grandmother finally gave up and took me to see Karola, a really close girlfriend. I was invited by her parents to stay the week.

Grandma handed me a *20 DM (Deutsch Mark)* bill, which was a lot of money and included *8 "DM"* for the train ride back. On Saturday we went all over town visiting friends, now involved in apprentice programs to became sales girls, bakers, mechanics, or prep school for higher education.

Karola, my friend, was learning to be a sales girl in a grocery shop, which entailed that she had to take the ice cream cart down to the soccer field on Saturday mornings to sell ice cream.

We did, and I made myself nearly sick sampling the different ice creams. Then Udo showed up, a former school mate, and asked if he could come to visit me, where I now lived. Sure, I told him, just write and tell me when and where. Then we planned to meet at the movie house the next day. This was a nice surprise. I had gotten over the incident where he called me a *"dumb goose,"* way back when I was a little girl. Now, I was 15 years old and appreciated his attention. He was rather good looking still, or maybe even more so than I remembered.

Before we went to the park, Karola, showed me where I would sleep and suggested to me "not" to take the money, the *20 DM*, with me. I might lose it. Then she showed me where I should hide it, under the bed, in one of her brother's bedrooms. She even supplied a billfold. So we went selling ice cream all morning, while my money was safely tucked away under her brother's bed.

When we came back I went immediately to check on my money and, guess what, it was gone. The billfold was there, no money inside. I was devastated, heartbroken. No money for the train home, no money for the movie the next day, with my friends.

Karola insisted somebody must have seen me put it here. Really, in her own house, a stranger? Actually she was the only one who knew where I put the billfold.

I had to tell her father who made me call grandma. Actually, I called our neighbor, we did not have a phone, and she had to inform my grandmother that the money was gone, just disappeared. How was I going to get home?

Grandma had me hand over the phone to Karola's father and instructed him to loan me the *8 DM*, which she would reimburse him as soon as I had gotten home, by money order.

That was that. I was more than broke. I wailed on and on and that was when Karola offered to pay for the movie, for both of us. "I pay for the movie tomorrow," she said in a most innocent voice, not blinking, totally unfazed, so she did. Now, wait a minute here! What is going on? My thoughts just scrambled, all mixed up in my head.

I remembered then, that we had discussed just a few hours earlier how she needed to get some money for the movie on Sunday. She had no money before I showed her my *20 DM*. Now, hours later, she had money for her own ticket and offered to pay for mine. I felt miserable! How could I voice my suspicion. I could not accuse her right in front of her parents, but all the circumstances pointed in one direction.

Oh, the misery I was in and what to do? If I had known what to call it then, I would have said I was having a full blown anxiety attack, besides being angry and upset. I knew what I wanted to do, but I had no proof and I had to make *"Gute Mine zum boesen Spiel."* Grin and bear it!

On Monday, her dad delivered me to the little train station, and made sure that I remembered to change trains twice before getting onto the one to Osnabrueck. This was the first time I had to travel by myself with changing trains. There was no "non-stop" ticket, because there was no connection to the bigger city except by *"Bimmel Zug"* (country train). Even once I got to a bigger city I still had to change one more time, otherwise it was more then *8 DM.* He was not willing to lend more.

The *"Bimmel Zug"* stopped at every small village on the way to the bigger city. It had bells to announce itself coming through, however slow. There was no rail road barrier to go up and down when passing over country roads. Cars, bicycles, farm vehicles just stopped and waited for it to pass. Bells rang and it slowly tracked by.

It took a long time to get to a bigger city to catch the *D-Zug.* If I missed the connection I had to wait around for another *"Bimmel Zug"* as long as it went in the right direction, sooner or later I would catch the right one. Karola's dad had told me "you are old enough, you will manage" and off he went, leaving me alone waiting for the right train. I made it home OK, stressed out, yes, but I made it home, four hours later.

Grandma waited for me at the station. I figured she would and I could unload the events of this disastrous trip, debate whether I was correct or way off base in this matter. Grandma told me there had been a rumor going around at the time we still lived in Epe, that

122

when Karola was around, money went missing, and that still continued into her time as an apprentice.

"Why had nobody told me" I asked? "Well, she was your friend and we did not want to repeat gossip, since nobody knew for sure. But it was wondered whether she might be a kleptomaniac." I did not know about it, nobody told me. That would have been good information to have. What do you think? What else did I not know about. I was 15 years old, and it seemed that life had just taken my blinders off.

My happy go lucky, blissful life, just existing in this bubble of childhood, had a crack in it. Is this how it would be, I would have to watch out, take care of myself, use good judgment, and where would I find that, I asked her.

"Tell me grandmother, where do I pick up good judgment?" It was up to me, what I made of my life, she said.

"Grandma, I don't think I like this!"

"Are you telling me that I am in charge of my life, whatever I need, I have to go after it myself? Is that right?" She looked at me and smiled.

" It's not so bad. We all have to get there at one time or another."

"What if I mess up?" I asked.

"Well, you just start over, just like I did."

All of this did not make me feel any better. I think I lost a lot more than a friend and *20 DM*. I lost a piece of my innocence.

This was my "coming of age."

Chapter 23

Gaining My Independence

What now, now that my blinders are off? The bubble in which childhood takes place had been cracked. To be clear, it seemed to have come off, altogether. What am I going to do now? What to do with my life? I have to provide myself with a  starting point. What will I learn? Who will push me into the right direction? I looked at my immediate family and could not see any help from that direction. They, mother and grandma, would not know what to do. Grandma was too old and totally involved in keeping me away from men, sort of like she had done with my mother, look what that had amounted too!

Grandpa was dead and no man in the house, except my uncles, who came around to find fault, to criticize, therefore not of any use to me, or would they be, if I asked them? What was wrong with them, anyway? How long were they going to blame everything on the war? It's not going to help me in finding out what to do, or where to go.

There was no enthusiasm in my family, not for any of my future plans. Oma always meant well, but meaning well is not helping me finding a job.

My two uncles had good jobs, so did their wives, but they did not help my mother to find a job; it was unlikely they would help me. Aunt Irmchen worked for a newspaper in Osnabrueck. She had to come across jobs, just by sitting so close to the news. They kept on pointing towards low education jobs, factory jobs, to be exact. I paddled between short time jobs suggested by my uncles. Nothing seemed to stick, hold my interest. I even started a job in a candy shop. It would have made me into a sales girl. One of my tasks was standing outside, in a costume, to offer candy to people that walked by. I did not care for it much. The second week the older sales girls shifted their jobs on to me as well, cleaning up after them, while they had coffee breaks. Then came cleaning the toilet and that was what broke this camel's back. I just walked out.

Then I got the idea to send mother off to inquire about different schools, but she came back with "too expensive." I don't think she really went to find out. She was fibbing, deliberately lying. It's disappointing to find out that your parent tells "white lies." Lies for their own convenience. I discovered later she did not believe I was serious.

Right about that time I found out there was money coming in, monthly. A check paid by the state for me, on account of being a war orphan. "Not bad at all." I made short order of that situation and confiscated it, with the understanding I could manage it myself.

"Jiminy Cricket, can you believe that?" I wonder what grandma was thinking.

However, it did establish some kind of beachhead for me. Sort of a small victory, really. "It was not small at all, come to think of it." The understanding was I had to take care of my own clothing and get

126

in line with some education. Grandma never discouraged me, whatever I tried.

I finally decided that I would go with my old plan to became a secretary, an office person, running an office, accounting, advertising, secretarial work. I had this in mind a long time, but they all talked against it. Even my last year in Epe, the school recommended I pursue a factory job, a sales girl apprentice, a baker, a seamstress or whatever was needed. The State had this plan to get young people interested in what they and the business community needed. "Sounds to me like outcome based education," or what they want to teach in school now as "common core," and that was some 50 years ago. However, Germany was moving into its economic miracle period, *"Das German Wirtschafts Wonder,"* that is what we called it.

I went into business college, taking English at Berliz on the side, also found a two year business apprentice position. All at the same time. Nobody would take anybody in their firm unless you had experience, typing and shorthand. It was not easy. In the apprentice program I learned just about every business method. Different ways money was handled between the European States. I often have thought that since it was a very small firm, I learned to run a business right from the start. I had to do all things, beginning with the mail, paying bills, writing letters, marketing and answering calls. You name it, this boss made me do it. It

came in very handy, years later. At the same time I studied in school, taking typing, stenography with Oma sitting there, every night, dictating from the newspaper, to help me increase my speed.

Uncle Willie would come by and see me practicing, remarking it was a useless effort, I would most likely not make it. "What a nincompoop," I thought. I would show him. I would show all of them.

" Oma, why is he so negative?" I asked her, "He sucks."

"The war" she said, always the war. Interesting enough, his disbelief in my abilities did the opposite for me. He would always mention that I would be just like my mother, turn up pregnant, somewhere down the line. I was getting fed up with him. He made me angry and often times he hurt my feelings. When least I expected it, he hurled an insult. He of all people should keep his mouth shut. I had enough "ump," unlike my mother, who folded up after being criticized. It did the opposite for me. Mother still would remark they, "her family, ruined things for her and now it was too late for her to learn anything new." She could have.

My uncles figured things out to their advantage. Why not keep an eye out for me? There was a true dislike from some of my uncles towards my mother, their sister, and by extension for me. I could have done it an easier way, straight into college. I found out later that the State would have paid for an education, if we had applied for it. Nobody did in my name. Nobody mentioned it. I don't know if they knew. I set off to do it my way, which was longer and harder as I found out. I don't think any of them were that ignorant. The one that told me about it, later, was Uncle Ernst, the one in French military prison. When he got out, he was the one who told me. I was already halfway through my program and I decided to finished it.

While all this was going on, I learned to dance, joined a dance finishing school and went dancing at 16 years of age, every Saturday

and Sunday. We could drink at 16 years, it was not official, but unless we were noticed for unruly behavior, nobody bothered. We stayed into the night. The only ones objecting, constantly, were grandmother and of course Uncle Willie, who seemed to have spies on us. He always came on Mondays to report that we had been observed. "Who in the dickens was observing us?" We never found out.

He reported that some of his friends had told Irmchen, his live-in girlfriend, that "we had behaved badly." That we were painted up, too much makeup, lips too red and dancing like *"Flitchen,"* floozies. It was the Twist, I think, we were dancing to. They had pretty nasty imaginations and Oma often fell into the trap and balled me out, when I came home late.

"It was pretty darn harmless, they just did not believe me, that's all!" I was too busy having fun to worry about Oma, except when she started to give away my stuff, like my bike, my movie star collection and started to call me names, "insinuating," that I was doing the dirty, the one of three things that surely would send me to hell, pick up a dreadful disease, or one could wind up in trouble. "We all know what that would be." She was pretty insistent in trying to find something that would stop me from going out.

To make matters worse, one Saturday afternoon, just when my Mother was giving me a new hairstyle for the dance that night, Uncle

Willie showed up. Observing what my mother was doing, he laid into her, called her names, accusing her of leading me down the wrong path, and had it not been enough that she turned up pregnant? Absolutely over the top and he kept on going with this. I was sitting on the chair, half finished with my new hairdo and here he was putting us all in a very foul mood. I did not really know that I could blow up like I did.

I told him "You shut up and mind your own business. My mother is old enough, has no husband, will not find one sitting at home. Where are you getting the idea that we, she or I, were out there, messing around?" I continued, "even if she did, she is single unlike you, you are married." By now he and Irmchen had married in a civil ceremony. "We all knew that you messed around, when you came to visit grandma in Epe, alone." Everybody knew it, so did I. "If you don't lay off, I will tell Irmchen, your new wife. What do you think about that?"

Boy, oh Boy, I guess that was a bit too feisty! I saw his fist traveling in my direction with a bunch of curses, I had never heard before. I responded with equal speed, scrambled off the chair, ducked, ran into the bathroom, locking the door behind me. Just barely, before his fists hammered on the bathroom door. Gee that was a close call. I had cooked my goose with him, that was for sure.

So much for that. I told grandmother, through the door.

130

"Get him to stop, send him away, or I have to crawl out the bathroom window, to alert the neighborhood. I am not going to be hit by him, like he hit my mother. If I yelled out of the window, how embarrassing would that be?"

That was the right bargain, because we did not want to be embarrassed, did we? I was told that often enough. I had already opened the window and spotted Renate, a girlfriend, on her way over to my place, to get her  hair fixed by mother, as well. Mother was making us look great and improved our teenage faces, with a bit of make up. You never look good enough at that age, I think. After my mother got through with us, we did.

She had worked a short time in Cologne, at the Ritz makeup company. It was famous for the production of the Cologne 4711, all kinds of lipsticks, plus make up. When she came back she brought tons of samples with her which lasted us for years, both of us.

Renate had just about made it out of her door, when I quickly told her my situation. I asked her to come around and make sure that the "luft was rein" the air was clean, meaning that the danger to me was gone, Uncle Willie had left. We were 16 years of age, Renate and I, on this fine Saturday afternoon in August of 1957.

If Uncle Willie was still hanging around, she had already instructed Hans, her cousin, to get a ladder so I could climb out of the 2nd floor window, in case I had to. After all I could not spend Saturday afternoon locked up. I also was a bit scared about having lost my temper, and what I had said to Uncle Willie. God knows, it might have consequences.

Question was, even if grandma sent him packing, what would she say to me? After all I had stood up to her son, my uncle. Never mind that all I said was the absolute truth. To hear it from a 16 year old was too much to swallow for this self-important man.

Grandmother took it well. I only remember she would give me a look sometimes after that, which I could not make out. Seems she was checking me out, trying to make up her mind about me. It almost seemed she did not mind at all, what I had said. At the time she just told me, "He's gone, you can come out now." She did not scold me at all. Nothing was said about this incident.

He did not come around for several weeks and daily life went back to normal. Whatever normal was at the time for three females with three generations between them. I think she didn't approve of his behaviors, but he was a man, and they lived by a different code. She did tell me that. She did not really approve of him having slapped my mother once in Epe after she came back from a dance, she was 24 years old already.

So life went on. I was pretty busy at school and all in all, I slowly gained my independence from grandmother. However, at times she would pitch a conniption fit, always about my going dancing and staying out late. I think she was spurred on by Uncle Willie, who now only came around when I was not there. That was a good thing, because I had enough to do with school the next two years.

Pretty soon I would have to come up with a mechanism to get grandma off my back; she would make these little sneak attacks. I tried to talk to her, but she was stubborn about it. I must make her understand that she was worried for nothing. How could I make her believe it. I had to think about it some more.

I did learn in school about "communication." I should try that on her, maybe I could get her to see, in my instance, that she was pretty much on the wrong track. I would not want to account for my mother on the same subject.

Okay, communication that was what I was going to use on her, but before I got to it, I stayed out again all night, dancing. This time I was not even home at 8 am, the next day. I had gotten a bit drunk, not too much, but enough to care less about when I should be home. I thought I was old enough by now.

Sunday morning, around 8 am, I was on my way home from an all night party, in a cocktail dress, no less, "dressed to the hilt." When I passed the local police station, one of the officers, hanging out the window, was taking a smoke.

He called out to me, " is your name Rosemarie?"

In surprise I said, "How do you know my name?"

He said, I just finished an incident report, fitting your description, *(mein kleines Spaetzchen)* my little bird, and "your mother just left here."

The nerve of him calling me *(Speatzchen)* meaning little bird, *(unverschaemter Kerl)* impertinent fellow, I thought.

Then he went on " Nice dress, are you going to church in it, by any chance?" He was mocking me! So ein ….. Well I had no time for him, or to figure out was he flirting or was he making fun of me. Still he was quite impertinent.

"No," was my answer. "What did you tell my mother?"

He went on with a big grin. "I told your mother she needed to wait 24 hours before she could file a missing person report. Also if we were having to look for all the 18 year old girls, missing on a Saturday night, we would not be able to do our jobs. Actually, we told the same to your Gandma, who showed up here at 4 am. We told her to wait and see if you were just out with your boyfriend."

"What? My grandmother was here?"

"Both said you did not have a boyfriend!" "Is that so?" the officer asked grinning all over his face.

"Really, is that your business?" I replied!

"Okay... Okay", he grinned, when I noticed he could hardly be any older than I was and having his fun with me. "Pretty bold". "This "Heini" (idiot), was flirting with me! He was teasing me in a very blatant way. I released a big sigh, that was all I needed, right at this moment.

Then he went on, " Where were you anyway," Not that it is any of my business, just curious, there is nothing open after 2 am."

"The Train Station Café," I said.

"Oh, he replied, I did not think of it, otherwise I would have send you mother down that way."

"Was zum Teufel" (what the hell), did you do there all night, you don't look drunk to me?", the young officer continued to inquire.

"I am not," thinking what a good thing that I was; sober, that is. If I had not been, the rest of my tipsy had left in a big hurry, as soon as I found out about the search party. I told him, "we sat around, telling jokes, just hanging out."

"Tell that to your grandmother," he continued, "she showed up here, loaded for bear. Became pretty insulting when we told her, we could not, or would not do anything at all, not tonight. The on duty sergeant threatened her with disorderly, if she would not calm down. Your grandmother was here at about 4 am and then she sent your mother, she just left. My advice is to get your little fanny home and if you hurry you will catch up with her."

"O shucks, what a nuisance." I took off my high heeled shoes, my feet were killing me, my silk stockings were ruined anyway, they had a run. I jogged down the street.

I really needed that communication session with grandma, pretty soon, this is getting to be embarrassing. The police knew me now, by sight, that is not good at all. I am getting a reputation, and for no good reason. Not that I did anything wrong, but it was never a good idea to be known to the local police. They would spot check the dance places, just looking for trouble makers; often the young English soldiers that were stationed here. We were under the British Occupation forces. None of the girls wanted to be caught up in one of these raids.

There was a certain caution to be had, they liked to quarrel and fight, so did the German boys I knew. They got upset if they thought we were being bothered by the English soldiers. The German boys would show up, offer to fight them off. I was told by one of my friends, Connie, that it was not a good Saturday night if they did not have a good fist fight going on.

Darn it, grandma was really turning into an nuisance. I knew she meant well, but regardless. I am tired of her looking

135

over my shoulder, and suspecting misconduct. This is 1959, I am almost graduated from school. I must try this communicating business, as soon as possible. Also I knew, talking things out was not her method, she liked to swing her fist, and ask questions later, if at all. Half way towards my place I caught up with my mother.

"There is no sense in fighting grandmother when she made up her mind about something," mother said. "So I went looking for you."

Just to be careful I sent mother into the house, just in front of me, and a good thing that was, grandma was there, with a wooden cooking spoon, ready to thrash me good. If she was mad enough she would. She started to hit and got my mother instead, because she was first in the door, "cracked her one," before I could grab her arms.

I held her, just hugged her tight, laughing I said "Grandma, I am 18 years old and you can't go off half cocked like this anymore. I am too big to be hit. I am going to bed to sleep, so don't fuss anymore. When I wake up later, we will talk. We will communicate, that is what I have been learning in class, lately. They say it works. You and I, we will hash things out, they say it's called communication. We will do it, I promise you, and "NO" I will not go to church to day. I will sleep first." Later, we did hash things out, and from then on we did a lot of hashing.

Chapter 24

Nichts Wie Raus Here (The Escape)

I could not wait to finally graduate and had made plans to get out and away, strip off all these restrains. I was being stifled. I could not get them to stop hovering over me. I could not be by myself for all the Tea in China, they, both grandma and mother, would show up and demand what I was doing, what I was thinking about. Good Grief! It got on my nerves. I wanted to be left alone, to think, to plan, to fantasize, to just dream of what was to come. I wanted to live, to experience life, to have the wind blow around my ears, to taste real life, to feel real love, even the pain, but nobody let me, they were hovering over me.

I was planning a trip to Norderney, a little island in the North Sea. This was a favorite vacation spot and I knew they would hire seasonal employees. I would plan on two weeks and then try to find a job, stay just for the summer. Grandma wondered why I was packing two big suitcases, for just two weeks. Little did she know. I was not about to tell her my plans, she was liable to find a way to stop me. No sir, not me, not with my plans for escape, finally.

Mother was too busy to really think about it for long. She had a job and a new boyfriend. I think I did hint around that I would stay for awhile, if I could find a job.

"Why did you go through all that studying," she asked, "now that you are finished, you throw it all away?"

"Oh no, mother, I am just taking time out, from all this domestic dominance. I am sick of it, don't you know it yourself? "How can I learn to be on my own, make my decisions, when you and grandma constantly interfere, not to mention your brother, Uncle Willie. I am sick of the entire bunch. I can't go to the bathroom without you all coming to check if I am okay, or what."

"But your education, you could get a real good job with it."

"I will, mother, when I am back. I will be back, you know, because it's just for the season." We are in the middle of this so called German economic miracle. "Grandma needs to know I will come in and out of her place, until I figure out what I will do with the rest of my life." I continued.

"Remember, my plan is to go to America."

She laughs at me then, and she giggled, "how will you do this." You don't know anybody over there that will sponsor you. You need a sponsor, like Manfred, next door, who went to Australia, but he is a mechanic and he is a man, they can make it everywhere. You are a girl. This is a pipe dream," she said. "You will not be safe there. They are all cowboys over there. You will not fit in. It is a myth to believe that the roads are paved with Gold in America." I informed her, that was for California, I had heard, and that was where I was heading, if I had any choice in the matter. However, now I was on route to Norderney.

I found a job within the first few days I was there, had not even time to enjoy the beaches, which were extremely windy and brisk. The wind would be too strong most of the time. I was hired into a milk bar as a waitress. I had never done this kind of work before. It did not matter, they trained us.

I stayed four months, through the season, and had great fun. I had found a small bedroom and I rented it. The weekly pay was just enough to supply the pocket money I needed to go out at night. Like all the vacation spots there was much entertainment going on. I was 19 in that summer of 1960 and everybody was smoking, and I set out to learn how. "Good grief!" I had to lay down on the bed to keep from passing out. It took a week before I was able to smoke in public, at night, when we were hanging out in those fancy dance places. Not one of my finer decisions in life, I think now, because it took me a lot longer to get rid of this awful habit.

We went sailing several times, but one particular time, the boys in charge had miscalculated their knowledge and I could see that they were scared senseless, so was I. They just could not turn the sail around to get it back to land. The tide was preventing us from bringing the boat back in. After hours of helplessly being tossed about, pulled back out to the sea, then pushed close to shore, but not close enough some of us decided to get into the water and swim to shore. We looked like drowned rats, cold and shivering, but we got the rent-a-boat guy to go out to rescue the rest of the boys. I was one of them that swam to shore since I was a good swimmer, but it was scary as hell.

The next trip was on a big boat, a day trip to an island, even further out in the Sea, which looked like a huge red rock sticking out of the Sea. It was called Helgoland. The Sea experience was not so great either. The Sea was so rough and wild that the entire group was sea sick, with that awful smell, inside the bowels of the ship. I believe the only ones not sea sick were the crew and the captain. Everywhere people heaving all over the place, unbelievable. I felt sick as well, however, I had not succumbed to  vomiting yet and hightailed to the top, being told by a sailor that would be the better position, to avoid the mess downstairs. I finally settled on the top deck, holding on to the rail in some corner.

Then we had to embark on small boots, waves splashing so high that we all got plenty wet. I don't know if that whole ordeal was worth the trouble. There was nothing on this island but venders and a few people that lived there. The approach and that huge red rock (the entire island was red), sticking out of the wild Sea, were the only interesting things. Nothing around but untamed Ocean.

In between all this, four months of wild dating. By the time the season was over, I was tired and ready to come back into grandma's safe haven, to rest up for my next adventure. Of course, after the money-order came for my ride home. I was broke again. Money was burning a hole in my pockets. The *150 DM* that I was still getting was only helping to stuff the hole for a short while, together with the weekly paycheck and the tips. I always seemed to be in a financial crisis.

Chapter 25

Panties on the Radiator

After I came back from Norderney I went to Duesseldorf and into a new job at a marketing firm. I followed Edelgard to the big city. I had left several jobs in Osnabrueck as a junior secretary because I was bored and the prospects of work in a big city was very exciting. Also I would not be totally alone because of Edelgard. We were into this *"German Wirtschaftswunder,"* the German economical boom, which meant jobs, as many as we wanted.

I took a job in a Marketing Firm, with contracts to get Gerber Baby Food, Stuyvesant cigarettes and some kind of French Cheese onto the German market. I am in; it sounded interesting. I reported to Fraulein Gertrude Maria von Trotzke, actually she was not just a Fraulein, she was a Doctor of marketing a real brainchild. Well, that was what she looked like, as well. Boy, here I am, stuck with *"Brunehilde."* She was extremely tall, dowdy looking, middle aged, glasses and her outstanding feature were the enormous boobies she sprouted and no bra to keep them in line, kind of hippie like. I was attached to her as her assistant, secretary and girl Friday. Little did I know of how many girl Fridays *Brunehilde* had gone through already, nobody stayed with her. She was different. Some would say, she was weird. I thought weird was interesting, at least I thought so in the beginning.

So we went out, every day onto the streets, with equipment lugged around by me, to interview the regular folks. A daunting task, very tiresome. Fraulein Doctor did the interview, I was right behind her taping the conversation and later typed it up. I had to make sense of the story, so she could analyze it.

I had majored in business, got my diploma working in a small marketing agency. But did I like this turn of events; all over the place, talking to strangers, right on the street business? I was not sure at all. She was always in flat shoes and a flowery dress which looked like a sack going down to her ankles. Like I said, she looked hippie, dowdy. If she would have had a flower in her hair, I would have been sure, but her hair was in a bun kept in the back of her neck. I wondered what her boyfriend looked like. She had one and was not shy of telling me all kind of details about him. He was a physicist.

She had an advanced degree in marketing, a doctoral, was thought of as brilliant, a creative genius, but the office staff was always gossiping about her behavior or her enormous boobs, which she managed to swing at whomever she was in conversation with. She was very creative in her work, with absolutely no common sense at all. She might have been around 45 years of age. It was hard to tell, because she did not use any kind of enhancement on herself and you could see that she neither shaved her armpits nor her legs, to the bemusement of the male personal in the office. And I had gotten stuck with her, oh, boy. She was not unfriendly, or even difficult, just down right weird. A bunch of very young, very highly strung artists, all over this office, after all this was a firm where one had to

144

come up with ideas, artistic ideas. Was she in charge? I don't think so, just enormously gifted and she assumed that position easily with her superior personality, not ever noticing every day concerns.

One fellow, Reinhard by name, was extremely bothered by her, I could see that. He seemed to get nearly sick when she approached him for work details. They called her *"Brunhilde,"* behind her back and when she came up behind Reinhard, he turned not only red but sort of purple. Somehow she would manage to lean over him, observing his work and her boobs, ever so slightly touched his back. Or it seemed they might touch him at any minute, however unintentionally. He would jump up, as if he got stabbed and rush away, with some mumbled excuse.

I have been watching and I can't wrap my mind around his behavior at all. He is young, maybe 22, just started working here. It seems that his hormones go haywire, overwhelm him, so he takes off. Somehow there is sexual electricity, when she comes up so close behind him, it translates for him into sexual arousal. Or maybe he is scared that she likes him, or something similar. Good Lord she is old enough to be his mother. There are other young males in the office, but none react that way.

I wonder if he is actually really that prim and proper or does he just find her behavior revolting, of which she is not aware off. I am not going to set him straight, it's not my job and he may think I might be interested in him, for involving myself. No Sir, I am staying out of this one, besides it's too much fun to watch. I believe Reinhard is a bit on the arrogant side with his good looks and his superior attitude of what he deems proper behavior. He is tiresome, to say the least.

Of course we all were watching for his display. It never failed, he would jump up and leave in a hurry, instead of politely telling her,

"Fraulein Doctor, please stop touching me. I don't like it."

145

It seemed to me that she was a touchy person, because when she was in a conversation, she would reach over and touch your hand, your arm and most of the people did not like it. I think that Germans did not like this familiar approach, at all. She was a strange bird, but harmless.

I was more bothered by having to participate in these sessions where I had to taste baby food, along with a bunch of young mothers and their babies. I had no idea about babies; they scared me. "How do you make them stop crying?" I would think when they all acted up at the same time.

Here we are, supposed to work together, but as soon as she enters the main office room, the guys flee the area, which made us late on many assignment when we needed their input. That was annoying. Then came the unfortunate incident and the office went on Storm watch. It had to be Reinhard, that discovered Fraulein Doctor's faux-pas (social blunder) in the community bathroom. He had found undies drying on the radiator. He stormed out, red faced and went straight up the elevator; up to the top brass, which resided in the very top of the building, to voice his protest. This was the height of brazenness and he could no longer tolerate her behavior. I saw Reinhard rush by and went checking. Sure enough, somebody had already gone into the bathroom and came out cracking up. He looked at me and said:

"She's got her undies in there drying off; I think she washed them!"

Fraulein Doctor enters the scene, grabs her undies off the radiator with the remark:

"Don't know what the hub-la is about, just a pair of clean undies!"

Apparently she had come down with her monthly, unexpectedly, no time to go home, had a flight late afternoon for a meeting in Italy. Her suitcase was already sent ahead. So she took care of her problem

146

the way she saw fit, not realizing that she might gross out the rest of her male colleagues. I was wondering, is she running around now without any underwear? I bet all the guys are thinking that, as well!

There was outrage by the male employees with Reinhard leading the posse. All the other times they had gotten so annoyed about her ways had now culminated in this one thing, "the panties on the radiator" absolutely unforgivable, and so they went on about it with absolutely no work being done that afternoon!

Then came the phone call from the top office, way on top. It was for me. It was requested that I be so kind and come up and speak to *Herr von and zu Hans Heinrich von Hirschfeld.* "Now what does he want with me?" I think, The boss was a *"Graf,"* a count, meaning he was of noble birth, with title.

I was ushered through the maze of different secretaries right into his office, where his "handsomeness" was holding court. He was about 35 to 40, sinfully handsome, very much aware of it and with a taste for sweet young things, as it was rumored. "God, I hope he does not think of me as his next conquest." I had only seen him from afar. Now how did this go again, "if he wants me to sit on his lap, it's time to leave."

"Fraulein Floreck, please come in, sit down. I wonder if you will be so kind to enlighten me. Tell me about the incident in your office, I believe I need your help!" My office? I don't have an office, I am kind of an underling, if you want to know the truth. I would have liked to tell him, but I kept my comment to myself.

"How?" I asked him.

"The undies on the radiator," he prompted me.

"Well, *Herr von Hirschfeld,* here is what I know," and I went to repeat what had happened. "I am only her assistant," you know.

147

"Yes" he replied "and the only one in that office that has not complained about her." He saw I was hesitating and he went on, "Please don't hold back. What do you think?" The Count went on before I could voice my opinion.

"You know," he said, "I can't do anything about Fraulein Doctor, she is our creative brain, and if that is not difficult enough, she is a relative on my father's side. It is extremely tiresome if I have to deal with them. I can't do anything on this end. What I want you to do is, talk to her, keep an eye on her. Can you do that?" he looked at me hopefully.

Gee, I had a hard time focusing on what he wanted me to say, or what I thought he wanted to hear. It was unsettling how handsome he was and he had a scar running along side one of his cheeks. That was from participating in the fencing sport and he got slightly wounded. A sport that the nobility frolicked in. Somebody must have bested him, hence the scar. It did not take away from his handsome profile. It just made him appear a bit reckless, a tad dangerous, I thought.

"Well," he interrupted my thoughts and I hurriedly responded.

"I can talk to her, I already have, but you have to do something for me also." I started to reply in a very careful way, hoping to find a way not to appears disrespectful.

"Well, go on," he said looking at me encouragingly. "You can speak freely, I need to know!"

"Okay, then this is what I think! That particular office has a bunch of highly temperamental men in it, very young, also very creative. You need to tell them not to be so darn sensitive. You are the boss and you tell them to cut out the gossip, to ignore her strange ways. Mention that, if you had to choose between them and her, you would pick Fraulein Doctor, because she has the brain power, has proved herself by the work she has done here! She has, hasn't she?" I looked at him questioningly.

He, this gorgeous man, looked up and grinned, then said "*jawohl*, I can do that, do you think these young bucks will leave?"

I shook my head and answered "Do you really care? They are a dime a dozen out there."

Then the audience was ended. I felt the shift in his behavior. I was being dismissed. I could feel it. It made me want to make a "*knicks*" bend my knees in a curtsy and move out backwards. But he got up, came around his desk took my hand, planted a proforma kiss on it. Just like in the movies when a gentleman takes a lady's hand to his mouth and grazed a "thank you" on it.

By golly he went and kissed my hand; I think I turned all red to my embarrassment and lost my voice for a second. "*Fraulein Floreck* I thank you for your input. I wish you a pleasant day." I was dismissed. I wonder if this was as good as being invited to sit on his lap? I think it was better!

Chapter 26

The Airplane Crash

It was the weekend and we were scheduled to go joy riding over Duesseldorf. It would cost *25 DM* per person. There were three of us plus the Yugoslavian pilot. He wanted to keep up his practice and over the weekend he rented a plane and himself out, for joy rides. The three of us, Edith, Manfred Fassbender and myself, were working in the Allgemeine Kranken Kasse, which would be like working for Oregon Health Plan, being that Germany has a socialized health care system.

We were going up on Sunday. Fassbender had secured the pilot, he was supposed to be good and a former fighter pilot around 36 years of age. We all were in our early 20s.

On Monday morning, when we stepped into the office, everybody stopped working, all went quiet in a very peculiar way. They stared at us, as if we were ghosts. Edith was right on my heels, but Fassbender had not yet shown up, he was scheduled in an outpost *(a Zweigstelle)* for this week. Edith a trainee for the civil service and I a junior secretary entered the work room which had about 40 people sitting on desks, working on cases. My desk and Edith's were empty, waiting for us.

The door to our immediate superior opened, he stormed out, having seen us through the glass window overlooking the work room. He proceeded to herd us straight into his office. "My God," Herr Schaefer, gasped, "You are alive!" "How wonderful, you are not dead. No names had yet been released, but it is all over the newspapers this morning and the radio. That plane you were on, crashed, nobody survived. We all thought that it was the three of you. What happened, who was on that plane if not the three of you?" he continued.

Edith, and I were stunned; we did not know what to say. I said "What are you talking about?" Herr Schaefer was the boss I fell asleep on, while taking dictation, only a few weeks ago. I had been shunned by him since that incident. He had not been too friendly towards me. I had been questioned by the Office Manager, Herr Rickenbacher, who was the top manager. I had to tell him that Schaefer's voice was so monotone, it put me to sleep. That incident just popped into my mind, when I looked at him curiously. I was surprised that he even cared, since I had become a *persona non grata* (unwelcome). Now Edith chimed in. "Are you saying the plane we went up in, crashed?" *"Ja, ja"* said Fraulein Habernack, the secretary, "it's been all over the news first thing this morning." She was the top manager's secretary, who had brought that news to Mr. Schaefers and like him, had observed us coming in. We, Edith and I, had no idea who those people were in the plane that went down.

We were here at work, and very much alive. Herr Schaefer, in a very precise fashion said. *"Also, erst mal langsam!"* "Slow down and tell us exactly from the very beginning! Tell us what happened and when did you fly?"

At that moment Edith and I looked at each other and started to go into shock, realizing what must have happened.

"Edith" I said, "were we not supposed to go up on Sunday?" "Why was it changed to Saturday, that's when we went up." "We went up with Dragur, the Yugoslavian, on Saturday." He called Fassbender, they changed it, because he could not make Sunday, something had come up for him. So we went a day earlier."

Was this pure luck or was it meant to be. By changing the day, we changed our luck, we lived? It was a scary thought. When we went up, it was fun, we did well, no problem with the plane, none that we, or the pilot, noticed. Good Lord, if we had taken the plane on the

day we were scheduled, it would have been all over for us.

I had to sit down and swallow that fact. It was too uncanny. To this day, I think I was spared, or that we had protection, that we were watched over. I never doubted after that time that there was a higher power, watching over me.

As for my new assignment: I was finally out of the dog house with Mr. Schaefer, but he did not take me back into his secretary pool. I went to Mr. Rickenbachers office, as second secretary for him and as help to Fraulein Habernack. I thought to myself that this new assignment could almost be seen as a small promotion, since now I was working in the big boss office, on the first floor. I never found out if they all thought of it that way, as a step up. I did, it felt better that way.

Chapter 27

It Was The Night of Carnival

I am back in Duesseldorf and work at the AOK *(Allgemeine Orts Krankenkasse)*, Germany's socialized health care system and insurance office. Germany had three kinds. One for the workers and trades people, one for the studied people and one for the rich, which was private, and paid for by cash money. I was a junior secretary, Edelgard a dental assistant at the AOK and Edith in a civil service training position. Brigitte, also living at Reckmann's worked for the banking system. Edith still lived at home.

Edelgard had found this place, the price was right, transportation, meaning streetcar, was close by. The Reckmann's were okay, reasonable landlords, especially Frau Reckmann. Except it was not allowed to have male company, so we had to sneak them up over very squeaky steps, in the dark, because the floor light was configured to last about 10 seconds, then one had to press again. It took 4 pushes on the light button to make it almost up to the attic. Up to the 4th floor and if you had to use the toilet you might as well use it before you got to your room. No sense in having to backtrack once you got comfortable inside your room. The AOK had public bathrooms where we could take showers or a bath.

Edelgard was 10 years older then all of us, had a steady boyfriend, Charlie by name. She was allowed visits, because the Reckmanns liked Charlie, who had been able to schmooze them. He was older, like Edelgard, had just graduated into an architectural firm, and was thought of as very suitable. Then there was Brigitte, she had the best room and was there the longest. She was also involved. I was a free agent, dated a lot but had a firm plan of going to America. Actually, come to think of it, I had one foot on the boat, for as long as I could remember. The Reckmann's had a grocery store at the bottom of the house on one side, kitchen and living room right behind it. However the bedroom was across the hallway, right next to the front door, where the stair case was going up. Outside, facing the front store, was a huge window advertising the wares. It was a small family grocery store, which sprang up on just about every corner in the city. There was a cigarette automate hanging on its side.

It was carnival season. We all had part-time jobs at night, making extra money. I had been in charge of the bar downstairs at the festivity hall of the *"Flederhof"* where the hard liqueur was sold. Edelgard worked upstairs in a spot where she could actually watch

the show and sell champagne by the glass. Her boyfriend would collect us after closing time to take us home by car. So it was arranged. Edith worked next to me in the bar and left earlier, she had found a ride home.

On this particular night I missed Edelgard and Charlie, I looked for them and could not find them, so I thought they took off without me, necking somewhere. I was tired, it was Friday night. I already had worked all day at the office. Maybe this was the true reason why I fell asleep on my boss, while he dictated, not just because he had that monotone voice. I did not have much sleep in those days. A lot of money was to be made, I needed money, more than I made at the AOK.

So here I was, unable to find Edelgard and so I took the last streetcar going in my direction. I did not dare to be stuck there, having to walk home. I had plenty of money, could have taken a taxi. I just did not think of it. A taxi would have been the right thing to do. I had over *800 DM (Deutschmarks)* in tips in my handbag. It had been a very lucrative night.

I got the last streetcar, got off at my street the Suitbertusstrasse, entered the street which lay dark and sinister in front of me. No streetlight at all to speak of, some very sparingly at long intervals. I went into the center of the street and proceeded down towards my house, glancing over my shoulder, or just plain turned around, to check if I could spot any danger.

I had a good grip on my handbag and made it to the house, key in hand. But as soon as I left the middle of the street, I heard a noise on my right side. I saw something white in one of the doorways of the houses I had just passed.

I hurried towards my front door, got there, took the steps two at a time, and that with my high heels. I made it. Inserted the key, pressed the door open, reached over for the light button. So far so good, I was in. But that was already the end of it. Now I could hear somebody running up, right behind me. I was still hoping, whoever was behind me was just after the cigarettes in the automate, hanging next to the grocery door.

No such luck! Now I could hear the steps coming up to the front door, from the outside, pressing against this darn door, not closing

fast enough. I myself was pushing against it from the inside. It was a magnetized door and would have closed all by itself, in time, left alone. That was its design. Now the door was experiencing pressure from both sides and did not move, had in fact stopped moving, leaving a small opening.

I had to stop pushing to reach over to activate the

light button. It kept going off, leaving me in darkness, with now somebody having partly squeezed through, his hands on the inside door. The door remained open just a spot, but enough. I spied a young man with a white straw hat and a red band in a beige trench coat. I battered his hand with my handbag, yelling, hurling every swear word I could think of at him, to no avail, he kept coming through. Then the light went out again, I had to stop pushing, to reach over for the light button. That is when he managed to push the door open, all the way, and slipped in.

It was a young guy drunk like a skunk. I could see that right a way, but that is not all I could see. His white trench coat had flapped open and I could see his *"hu hu"* out of his stall, thrashing all over the place and him making hand movements. He seemed to think this would entice me. What it did, was to scare the hell out of me. I started to yell and scream in earnest now. The swear words were just coming out of my mouth.

"Du Drecksack, (dirt bag) get the hell away from me," all the while I was swinging my heavy handbag at him, hitting him.

Then I started banging on the back side of the hall wall, knowing that the Reckmann's had their bedroom right behind it. Normally I would be extremely quiet, getting into the house at this late hour, not trying to make any undue noise. But this was different, I needed Herr Reckmann now, in PJ's or not. He was a scary looking dude, he would make short cakes of this *"Dumpkopf."* So far my hitting and yelling seemed to have only made him more determined. He now started pleading with me. All the while I just kept hitting him with my bag.

Now I could hear a rumbling next door, finally I had gotten old Herr Reckmann's attention, his head popped out the bedroom door demanding, "what in the world is going on here?"

But no sooner had he said it, he had appraised the situation and he was out the door, PJ's and all, looking like an angry old grizzly, charging after the young guy, who barely managed to slip out the still open door and run off.

Frau Reckmann was out now as well, however she had managed to put on her robe. I had sank down the wall and sat on my haunches, clutching my handbag to my chest, I was shaking, and that quite a bit.

"Why are you alone?", demanded Herr Reckmann. "Where are Edelgard and Charlie? Why are you running around, alone, in the middle of the night?"

"They left without me, I could not find them." I defended myself.

"The light is out on the street," Frau Reckmann said, "I called the city, twice, on it."

"Regardless, young ones have no sense at all. You talk to her and no more of this nonsense. I am going back to bed, I have got to get up again at 4 am, to open the shop," Mr. Reckmann said and went off to bed.

"It's not my fault, that this idiot tried to assault me," I said. "What was this all about, somebody better tell me. Why did he acted like an idiot and scare the dickens out of me?"

Right about that time a car stopped in front and Edelgard got out, came up the stairs, and scolded me for having left.

"I left," really, "You were not where you where supposed to be!"

Frau Reckmann herded us into the kitchen, behind her grocery store, where she made us hot chocolate and we debated who was at fault, and why men behave the way they do, among other things.

"No, I did not recognize that young guy as one of the customers of the bar, really, he was not in the least familiar to me!" I replied after being given the 3rd degree by both Edelgard and Frau Reckmann.

Only Frau Reckmann knew that we, the girls, were working in the carnival season. Her husband, a very religious man, was not informed, he would have had a conniption fit, had he known. He had a Monsignor in his immediate family, which signifies a priest honored by the pope.

After that we, Edelgard and Frau Reckmann had a pretty good information session on how to stay safe, if that was even possible. On what men do when they got drunk, their needs, justified or not, just so I would know what to do, if I had a drunk boyfriend on my hands, etc., and so on.

"Well really, I did not know this guy and I don't date guys that get drunk on me in the middle of a date." However this need thing. I did not know about that, not until tonight. I thought it could be controlled? And anyway I had been more worried about the money in my bag. I was not about to tell them, how much I had in that bag. Loose lips sink ship? However, that was my lesson for this month, I think?

Chapter 28

Paris-France

Paris, France my first trip out of Germany, five glorious days and four nights in Paris, by bus at *100 Deutschmark,* that was cheap, even then. (Translated about 25 Dollars) The bus went over Aachen into Belgium then France, on to Reims then Paris. We lodged in a small hotel, only minutes away from the Gar du Nord and the metro. At night we could hear the trains rattling by, shaking the armoire. The room was small, one full bed and in front of the bed a toilet, at least that's what it looked like, kind off. There was no water sink in the room, but a strange looking toilet. Different rules for different folks, I thought. Although I was not sure I wanted to use that in front of my friend, Edelgard.

Yes, I think it was a foot washing-massage device: it was spouting warm water, when I turned it on. Oh good, my feet were killing me!

They always did because I wore high heeled shoes, nothing but high heeled shoes. I had to be in style, you know!

Edelgard had gone out onto the corridor to check the proximity of the bathroom and the rooms of other friends, then we were going to take off to look around. I had thrown my shoes off and stuck my feet into the bowl. The warm water spouted out, ever so gently over them. It seemed it was giving my feet a little massage.

Okay, that was it, it's for the feet, it works well that way. Just what my feet needed, right about now. So I thought. The French have it figured out, they have foot massages in the hotels, what a great idea. I looked around and it was a rather plain room except for this fancy foot wash-massage basin, so close to the bed, that I sat on the bed, easily, with my feet inside the device.

When Edelgard came in, she died laughing,

"Do you know where you have your feet in?"

I looked at her in surprise, as she was lying on the bed, not able to catch her breath.

"It's a bidet" she said, "and not for washing feet. Definitely not for washing feet."

"What is a bidet?" I said.

Edelgard was still laughing, rolling around on the bed.

"It's to rinse you after sex, or before sex, or to stimulate! Naturally it would be kept right next to the bed. You are such a *Dummkopf*, a pinhead, a baby!"

"What?" I called out, " Really?"

I lifted my feet out; then I thought about it. "So what, it feels good on my feet" I did not live that incident down for a long time. It was

164

the joke of many a day, the boys teased me for being so naive. Well, how was I supposed to know about a "bidet," never heard it mentioned at home, it was not standard bathroom equipment in German households. We were lucky if we had a tub in the bathroom, let alone a thing to wash your "you know what" in.

On the bus we had befriended two boys and one more girl and the five of us went all over Paris on foot. We went to all the churches. The church of Les Invalides where Napoleon Bonaparte was buried, Sacre Coeur, dedicated to the secret heart of Jesus, Notre Dame Cathedral, the Arc de Triumph, walked along side the Champs Elysees, to the Louvre, "the Palais Royale," now a museum hosting so much art that it would take weeks to see them all. We had decided to go for five major pieces of art in the Louvre. Naturally the Mona Lisa, the Venus of Milo, the armless winged Nike of Samothrace, and a few I can't even remember. The Palais de Louvre is where the French Kings reigned.

On one night we went to Montmartre, the Moulin Rouge, (the red windmill). We had enough money to see one cabaret show, up in the rafters, a neck breaking undertaking, to even get up there. But the view was great. Onion soup after that, then on our way home to the hotel, by foot. We got lost, so we went into every little bistro for directions. We did not get out before we consumed a French green drink. A small schnapps glass of aperitif, a licorice flavored liqueur. We got home that night, very early, but not before we wound up at the fish-market; the very famous French fish-market; one could smell the fish a mile away. That's how we knew we were at the fish-market.

We had a baguette, still warm, with cheese and some wine for breakfast, while we were trying to find our way home. I was barfoot again, high heels are never suitable for long excursions. But I had to look fine and so I had high heels on, matching my suit. The shoes came off on the way home, it never failed.

Not much sleep that night, or morning, we tumbled on top of each other in that French full bed, it had a hole in the middle, from too much use, it was old. Then, as one of the trains rattled by the armoire shook and leaned towards the bed; so I jumped out to catch it before it fell down on the bed. We moved it to the side and later back into place, before we left the room. There was really no more sleep that day. Soon we were up and ready for our next sightseeing.

Off to Versailles just a short ride by bus. Here Louis and Antoinette lived before they were taken to the guillotine and their heads lobbed off. The garden was wonderful, the inside full of golden rooms, the most famous the mirror room. And how they lived, while their people were starving. Here Antoinette uttered her most famous sentence, when told that her people were starving and had no bread; she said *"then let them eat cake!"*

Eiffel tower, I climbed up, by foot; there was no elevator. I went to the top, inside Mr. Eiffel's office and looked at all his designs on display. The view was astounding, all over Paris. When I came down I spotted a stand which advertised "hot dogs", which in German translation would mean *"Heisser Hund."* Never had one of those! I went to inquire whether or not I would be served a dead dog? I was safe, just a bun with a wiener in it, *"a wiener wuerstchen."* Interesting, they called it a hot dog.

On the last day we went off to find the famous Flea Market and if possible check out the crap holes, used in olden times, before the toilet was invented. It had a room with one or more hole in the ground and one had to crouch down to do it, not that easy either. It was a messy undertaking to say the least. We peed over our shoes. The smell in there was something else, too. I think they kept it as a tourist attraction, because the restaurant was well known to have a *crap hole*.

Edelgard was supposed to have some knowledge of French, from school. We ordered food, we could not just go in there to look, we had to order, so we did; it was nothing we could recognize. No idea what it was. The boys ate it anyway, I could not get it down.

The flea market, what a mish mash of people from all kinds of nations. Never had I ever seen so many foreign people, plus what was sold, unbelievable, then the different languages. It was something!

Now, however, I started to notice that I got stared at, not in a good way. I was very blond, very young and my friends had to take me in the middle of our group. Somebody pinched my butt! There was a lot of attention by some of these strange looking fellows. Some had turbans on, some had Muslim head scarfs, with wild looking eys, staring at us; or me, I could not really tell. My friends thought they were staring at me, hence they took me into their middle of our little group. We heard of cases, where young girls were kidnapped right off the street, in broad daylight, and never heard off again. There was a well organized trade going on, well advertised, well spoken of, even by the police.

Not the first time that a young women, alone, had been grabbed off the street and sold into a harem, never mind that this was Paris and not Marseille. Young men were advised to be careful as well. If they were unlucky and got drunk in one of the taverns, they found themselves on a boat from Marseille to Algiers, having signed papers, while drunk, enlisted into the French foreign legion. It happened to somebody my grandmother knew, when she was a girl, back in Strasbourg. There were times when one year the region was German and the next year it was French again. The military was always looking, and not always in the legitimate way.

But back to the male Parisian, it seemed that no matter where we went, the bus, the metro or by foot, we the girls got attention from the males, who flirted outrageously. You could not even glance at them; they seemed to believe that was a "go ahead" kind of signal. The men were complimentary, they would look at you, try to get your attention, turn around and follow, hoping, you would respond to their flirtations. Parisian men, "I think they put something into their water supply." It must be, we joked about it a lot. No matter were we went, metro, everywhere, even in one of those self service eateries, you could not look at a guy, without them taking it as an invitation. I had never had that much attention paid to me, ever, as over those five days.

"It felt great to be a girl, wonderful." No wonder people speak of French men having a reputation of being great lovers, always adoring women, no matter what age or what you looked like, it seemed. It was extraordinary. No matter how old the woman was, no matter how young the guy was, there was a perpetual flirting and adoring going on. In the eatery, I swear, there was a kid, maybe 13 or so, who eyed me and started flirting. Extraordinary, especially compared to the German men. I wonder if now it would be considered harassment, it would be a shame, come to think of it, if that would be the case.

Chapter 29

Palma de Mallorca-Spain

Three full weeks on Mallorca-Spain. It's an island in the Mediterranean, off the coast of Spain; the language is Spanish. Edith made the reservation; we had made tons of money in the carnival season. I had already gone to Paris with Edelgard and now this trip. This was a real vacation and planned for three weeks. All of it in the sun, which was sparse in Germany.

I was also back with my private English teacher, Fraulein Ruehl, who spoke six other languages besides English, three times a week. We would proceed as if I came to her for high tea, then made conversation, all in English. She was very good, gave me a lot of pointers and she must have been at least 80 years old. She never married and now lived with her brother's family.

I was still working for the AOK. Now that carnival was over I had taken on a night job in a grilled chicken place, making extra money. Twice a week, Edelgard and I went to substitute when the regular waitress was gone. We made good money. I had lots of plans, including now this Mallorca vacation.

The trip to Spain was a full service accommodation, breakfast, lunch and dinner included; the beach was call Arenal, the Hotel of all things "The San Francisco." Was that an omen, or what? The air plane ride was my first trip on a big airplane. Well it was kind of big, so I thought, it was one of those charter flights. The trip destination was Mallorca and everybody went to the same spot, different hotels, but still same spot.

The plane had about 150 passengers and it was a little biddy dingle-a-ling kind of a thing. I felt every movement of it; very bumpy. I thought that was supposed to be that way. It was a little bit scary. We made it okay, in about 4 hours, now it would be 2 hours anywhere in Europe. It was a charter flight, all right.

Our hotel was great, right on the beach, just separated by a street one had to cross to get to it. However we were advised, never to do that in a bathing suit, always dressed, undress on the beach. It was the custom, just as you never entered a church without covering your head.

We spent our days mostly on the beach, 8 hours in the sun. We took trips to Palma de Mallorca, the main city, toured it. Not much to see otherwise. We took horse back riding. The boy that taught me to ride, was my boyfriend for a few weeks; we actually tried kissing from horse to horse. A bit complicated, but It does work. We went dancing at night, had made friends nearly the same day, male friends, that is. Edith was already sort of engaged back in Germany, but she caroused plenty; I guess it was her "good bye to single-hood." My entertainment was nothing to write about, nothing that excited me greatly, I was pretty picky.

170

We could have lunch or dinner in the hotel and found out quickly not to have wine with lunch because it would ruin the entire afternoon. We watched and saw how other people mixed their wine with water. We did not at first and found ourselves blitzed right after lunch. Then we started mixing the wine as well and it lost the wine taste, yet it was not water either, rather it had a vinegar taste. There was nothing else to drink except water, straight out of a bottle, like Perrier. We were not experienced travelers, dinner was interesting, very Spanish, not really our taste; it had a show attached to it and naturally a dance at the end of it.

When I finally got home my grandma closed the door in my face saying "I am not buying anything" pretending I was a sales person. I was so tanned she did not recognize me. At least that is what she implied, or pretended. My hair, formerly blond, was bleached white from the sun and my skin was brown.

Chapter 30

April 24, 1963 Going to England

I am going to England. I am going to practice English for six months. At least that is the plan. I finally found a placement company that arranged for young women to go to different countries in Europe as I found out, also to the USA. I am going to go to America. It's been my dream since I don't know when. I decided to go to England first because the president of the US

was assassinated, it scared me. What am I supposed to think about that? Unthinkable really!

There are other reasons also, deep inside me. One is that I want to live life, experience things, be part of adventures. The world is full of adventures; I want to claim my share of living them. It seems I really have not lived life, or what is supposed to be my life, so far. I live in a cement jungle in the city, mostly damp, cold, gray and dreary.

Would I have the courage to go, this time? I want to feel love, hunger, pain, even love lost, as long as it was there to begin with. I knew nothing of any of it. I feel like a page with no writing on it. I want to travel, see the world.

I am going to plunge into life. When I was 19, just out of school, I took off for 6 months, it was a glorious adventure. I spent four months on Norderney, an island, off the coast of Germany, a favored vacation spot.

Now my bags are packed again and I am on my way. Nobody could understand why I was going, or agreed with me, for that matter. Only Oma said nothing, just listened to me, my dreams and plans. All around me my girl friends are getting married, worrying about becaming old maids. Edelgard was now engaged, she finally had landed Charley. I was glad for her; I was glad for Edith, also, who now was pretty much involved, with Dietrich, whom she had met during the carnival season, not long ago.

My train leaves in 30 minutes, but I am still not dressed. Edelgard, nervously patrolled, the corridor, outside my room, at Reckmann's, to bring me to the train station. I left my room; totally messed up, for Edelgard to clean up, which I knew she would.

I got to the train station just in time for the connection to Cologne, to meet up with the group of exchange students, en route for England. We were going from Düsseldorf to Cologne, then Cologne to Dover and cross the Channel to London.

Six weeks in London. The arrangement in London was that we were to be settled into an English family, mostly teachers, for room and board, while going to school. After six weeks our final destination was West Scotland, placement as au pair in a youth hostel, again for room, light work while practicing English.

It was scary, because I did not know the girls, the organization and who would meet us, get us onto the right boat or who would pick us up in London. My English was very limited. I just could not wait any longer. I had to get on with learning to speak English.

In Cologne I stood in the train station, and watched the trains moving in and out. I am trying to spy who might be from the same group. Where was the sign, supposedly it said "Norwegian Youth Association." I approached a very young girl with stringy, blond hair that fell all over her shoulders, with dark, black made up eyes, that looked to me like she might be a student. I was right. She was Hella, 18 years old, studying to be an actress. She was as skinny as a bean pole and extremely outgoing. We had the same destination, at least as far as London.

I breathed a sigh of relief. But was that all of us, I was thinking, no more then two girls? I worried a bit, you heard all kinds of dangerous things. But it was too late; I could not possibly turn around. I also was thinking that I never done any house work, ever, and would I be able to do it. Well how hard could it be?

Finally a train, the right one, pulled up which stated "Reserved for students." Still we had not seen the student guide that was to meet us. No sign of him, for the entire time we waited in the station, next to the correct train tracks. Finally we got into the train, convinced that it was the right one, it said Dover-London on it.

Our coupe' was locked and we waited in front, looking out of the window for our travel guide to appear. Finally I spied another girl that belonged to our group by the name of Claudia. She was very pretty and had a very long blond pony tail. I remembered, sorrowfully, that I should never have cut my hair. I got it cut at 15, wanting to look grown up. Too bad I never had anybody to talk some sense into me.

Then we spotted him, our guide, he was a very young man, nerdy looking, with red hair, an arrogant face, with a white armband that identified him as guide. He absolutely paid no attention to us, whatsoever, climbed in and out of the train, checking us one by one, without saying a single word.

Meanwhile, another girl showed up. Her name was Erika and she came from Berlin, born in India, whose parents were diplomats in state service, stationed in India, where she learned English. She wore glasses and kept removing them constantly. She felt self-conscious with them on. Erika and I had the same destination, yet we were housed with different families in London for the first week.

I was hoping to meet up with the girl that I would be quartered with and together we would try to find the address. Up to now she had not arrived. The guide stood outside the train looking in one direction, as if he was waiting for the rest of us. He had not asked us a single question and did not assign us our seats.

All of a sudden another man showed up, older maybe around 35 to 40. He got into the train, opened up our coupe' and seated himself on one of the window seats, placing his brief case on the opposite window seat, which shortly was then occupied by our very disinterested guide. We inquired if we could now be seated and when no negative motion was noted, we all filed in and took a seat.

What a strange bunch of people. How are we going to get to the correct places and addresses in London, without getting lost. None of them said *"Guten Morgen"* or Hello. As soon as the guide got in, he took the opposite window seat, opened up the brief case, got out a good sized lunch box and started to munch on his food.

I had not thought that much into the future, what I would eat, thinking we would have a restaurant car in the train. Not so. Later we

jumped out at different stops, dashed to the candy automates, to get some provisions. In Dover we were told we would have a longer stop while the train was transported onto the ferry for transfer to England. That turned out to be only partially true.

I started a conversation with the two girls and soon found out that both had quite a lot of English in school, in comparison to me. I just had a few classes and in the end I had private lessons by an old German school teacher who spoke six languages. I had been enrolled in the Berlitz school. Also Fraulein Riegel had given me private English lessons, to boost my speaking, but it had not kicked in yet. I knew I was in for a swim or sink lesson in English.

Before middle school and my apprenticeship my grade in German spelling was not high enough for them (school) to let me take English, which was highly annoying to me. I just learned it on my own. It was not true either! Fraulein Wiedemeyer did not like me, I was too mouthy, so she marked me down, just enough, to miss getting into the English class. I found out when I asked for another copy of my grade and noticed that on that copy, she had marked me higher which would have allowed me to be in the English class. To be told that I couldn't learn something was reason to show them I could.

177

I was thinking how the last year in school they tried to push girls into jobs that the systems needed filling, per family work history or what the industry needed, because my mother worked for a spinning factory, it was thought, I should work in a factory, as well. Or maybe become a sales girl behind a counter selling candy, groceries or likewise in a department store. Except it was not really a big department store, just like a mom and pop store. I was rebellious and took control of my own life at about 15 years, when I noticed that nobody (not my mother or grandma) had any ideas or suggestions.

In my family the gene pool for college graduates were slim pickings. That mattered a lot when it came to higher education. If you had no direction, early on, it usually did not happen. I made it work, because I was obstinate. I realized over and over again that I should have gone to college the regular way. There was nobody to explain it to me. I just wanted to be working as a secretary in an office. I could have still done that, after college, yet I would have had a formal education in one piece, instead the hard and long way I went. So these girls had a bit more knowledge of English and I hoped I would catch up in the six weeks in London and later in the six months in Scotland.

I was hanging on to my thought, off and on, while Hella spoke without pause to both men. That prompted the older fellow to start pointing out points of interest outside, as the train steamed by the countryside. He was practically a life history book and very happily gave up his knowledge. Hella and Erika were fascinated by his lesson, traipsed back and forth after him, when he decided to also explain points of interest on the other side of the train. He was happy to part with his knowledge.

I stayed put in my seat, eyes closed and let my thoughts wander towards my adventures and what I would find, when I got there. I did not sleep much the night before and was tired. I thought they would transport the train onto the ferry in Dover with us on it. "Not so." I went to the bathroom and before I got back, the train stopped, all had departed, I had lost them in the crowd.

I had to squeeze myself through the people, suitcase in hand. I could only see the blond, stringy hair of Hella, in the distance. Our guides, both of them, were gone; I never saw them again. I just moved into the direction I had seen that tall bony art student disappear, hoping, that sooner, or later I would catch up with them.

So I did, I found them again at customs, on the border. I never saw such a multitude of people of all cultures, in my entire life. Languages I did not even try to figure out, where they might belong to, what country, I mean.

The train got loaded up, but those with suitcases had to go on to customs for passport control. After that we trotted off towards the ferry. We could not find a seat, the boat was full, we had to find an empty spot on top, the open deck, and parked ourselves. Erika had already stopped two young boys, with whom she was happily conversing in English. It was cold, wet and windy and we were all glad to finally get on land in England. Here too was a great mass of people. Again we had to go through customs, where once in awhile a "bobby" picked out a person for further health examination. We inquired, actually, we sent Hella, the art student, off to the front to find out, "why?" It was a health check. If the doctor thought somebody was ill, they would be detained. What they would do with them, who knew? It would make us miss the train and we wanted to stay together.

By this time, after hours on an open boat, through the channel we all were sneezing and starting to cough. We sucked on cough candy as not to get noticed. I was lucky, even so, by this time I was pretty much coughing. I had a real cold coming on, plus I hardly could swallow, but we got through without being noticed.

Hella had found a young man to carry her suitcase, lost track of him with her suitcase and had to search for him after we got out of customs. She got separated from him plus suitcase. When she noticed, she just dropped her purse and took off back into customs.

She had dropped her purse, right in front of us to the ground and ran off, in search of this guy with her suitcase. We got stuck with her purse, waiting desperately for her to return, so we could get on the train from Dover to London. We could not leave, because we had her purse, with her money, and she was out there looking for the young guy that had helped her. Somehow they got separated in customs, which was no wonder with these masses of people.

We could not leave her purse on the ground, nor could we leave with it. What a scatterbrain this girl was. We had to let the first train go. Finally she showed up with her suitcase. We scolded her for letting her suitcase out of sight. Two hours later we got to Victoria Station in London. It was dark.

Now began the task of figuring out how to read the subway instructions and in what direction I needed to go. I did not know how to operate the darn telephone to call the family to tell them that I had arrived and needed to be picked up. Hella tried to phone for me but it did not work. Who knows, maybe I did not have the correct change, maybe we did not know how to operate this public phone.

Hella just stopped a guy again and asked him to telephone for us, which he did. The telephone worked for him. My landlady spoke no

German and I spoke very little English. This is going to be interesting.

Again Hella stopped a guy, right on the street, asked him to help me to get to the correct subway entry, and into the correct direction. She seemed to have no problem enlisting, young, good looking men, blinked her painted black eyes and "whoop ti do," here we had help again. "I need to pay attention on how she did this for future moments." I would probably be too embarrassed to use this method, I thought.

Well, this young man even tried to carry my bag and almost fell over. He asked me in broken German

"*Was is da drin, Steine?*" What's in there, rocks?

I laughs and said "No just stuff."

He took me quite a ways: after 5 corridors, 3 stairs and down a long hallway and he delivered me to the right ticket place, where I was able to get a ticket by just showing them the address.

Nobody understood my English. I was able to read the different stations, went up the escalator, never been on one before, and finally arrived in the correct train station, got out on Charing Cross and was finally at the teacher's house at 9:30 at night, exhausted and exasperated.

My landlady was very tall, slender, about 45 years of age, with a very wrinkled face, red lips and red powdered cheeks. Her English sounded as if she was singing it, I understood nothing, whatsoever. She gave me a tour of her house, introduced me to two girls, who were still living here, for one more week. Monica and Ingrid.

My first questions was "*Sprechen Sie Deutsch*" Do you speak German?

They were laughing out loud and I fell into the next best armchair. Now I found out that both had one more week of stay, before I was

181

placed with this landlady. I needed to be transported, yet again, to a different family for this week, then back here.

Most likely this was all a booking misunderstanding. Nothing was ever simple here, I found out soon enough. Mrs "B" made tea, we waited for the other girl, my roommate for this week, so that we could all go together. I was glad I did not have to find my way to the other family tonight, alone.

The girl we were waiting for was Renate from Frankfurt. Apparently we all came from different parts of Germany, arrived not only at different times, but also by different means. We waited until 10:30 pm but she did not show up. The girls took me to the new address. They had to make sure that they could catch the last bus back here.

What an ordeal. We took the bus, changed twice to different buses and after 45 minutes, we got to Newbury station. I was totally lost by now. It was dark, I could not remember any points. Everything was so different, so strange, so not German, I was too tired to even care. At the house of this landlady, we could not find the bell. The door did not have one, it had a knocker.

The door knocker you had to lift up, then let it drop on the door. It made a good noise. Finally the door opened and the girls explained to her, in English, who I was. Her name was Mrs. Web and I had to stay with her one week.

The girls left and Mr. Web managed to get my suitcases up the small, narrow steps. You could only go up or come down one at a time. Mrs. Web was a quick, little person and very friendly. The entire household was very (buergerlich) middle class. She had two daughters and was only in this house for a short time. Everything looked new and fragile in pastel colors. The corridor was light blue. All was very dainty, reminded me of a dollhouse. I could imagine that by the next storm, the windows would be flying out, over the roofs. The walls seem to be very thin and I had the feeling that even if you whispered, one could hear it all over the house, or maybe even in the neighbor's house.

Mr. Web had a special room for the TV, which had only chairs, a small table for the ashtrays and a fireplace. Actually, the house had two fireplaces. Later I observed that I never saw a house in my time in England that did not have a fireplace. However, these two were only make believe fireplaces and housed electric heaters.

I was cold, very cold, and with dismay I thought what it would feel like to stay a winter in these dainty little houses, without walls, without stable windows. It must be a ready made house. The windows were out of metal material for sure. Not that I did not like it, I liked it fine, I was just so cold that thinking these thoughts make me even colder.

Every room had a carpet from corner to corner. Mrs. Web tried to find out if I was hungry and brought me a glass of orange juice. We sat in the little TV room, tried to make conversation while we were waiting for Renate. She could not understand why I was only there for one week, I could not clear it up. All I did know was that she was further away from the school, I was to go to, I could walk to it from Mrs. B's house. We called her Mrs. B, because her name was long and complicated.

At 12:30 pm Renate showed up. She had been one of the people delayed at the border in Dover, hence her late arrival. She got picked out of the mass of people, by a "bobby," what they call their policeman, to see the doctor at random. She spoke better English, also with a twang of Frankfurt. She spoke English better than I that was all that counted.

She turned out to be a very tall, dark blond girl with big feet and huge boobs. She was hard of hearing and sometimes could hear absolutely nothing. She had 8 operations on her ears. When she did not look at you, straight away, she missed you addressing her and would not react. She was very goodhearted, always trying to help somebody out.

She was what I would think of as a hippie. She hitchhiked with her backpack, flat shoes, all over Germany, whenever the opportunity presented itself. She planned to go to Africa as a social worker, after her time here in England. She took her studies in a bible college and was to join her boyfriend in Africa to work.

Later, she never wanted to join any of us to go out for fun. I caught her often just looking into the air, her thoughts somewhere else, maybe with her young man. Well, as soon as Renate arrived, Mrs. Web produced a full dinner in the middle of the night, which we had to eat. Actually it was more like what we would eat at midday in Germany. We usually eat light at night, nothing at all in the middle of the night. We had cornflakes, potatoes, salad, sauces, sweet deserts and tea of course. We ate to make her happy.

Then we went to bed and there was only one blanket to cover us, not the warm feather beds, like in Germany. I was freezing, wondering, if I would be frozen stiff in the morning. My first day in England, what a culture shock. Never were things so different.

Chapter 31

Day Two in London

When I woke up, not frozen stiff, we went down for our first English breakfast. Corn-flakes, fruit, bacon, sometimes an egg, toast and orange marmalade. This turned out to be similar ever day. Not German at all.

After breakfast Renate and I went on our way to meet up with the other girls. Our room and board, however temporary, was far away from school. It took us 2 different buses to get to Tooting Bec, where in a week from now, we would be housed. From there we had to take the subway to Victoria Station. We made a date with Erika, to meet there to go to visit Madame Tussauds Wax Museum. We were late, the girls had left. So we bought post cards and stamps instead, then embarked on the way towards school on foot, hopefully in the right direction.

Our sense of direction now in the daytime was good. Pretty soon we saw Big Ben and Westminster Abbey. This was the church where kings and queens were crowned and many were buried. Mary, Queen of Scotland, was buried there, plus a bunch of counts, kings, statesmen and poets. Big Ben belongs to the parliament building. Big Ben is noted to have the most famous bells in the world. For sure it was one of the famous signs of London, next to the tower bridge. We went past Big Ben, towards the St. James Park.

London has many big parks, gigantic green areas with little ponds, fountains, cafes (self serving) and opportunities to ride horses. St. James Park runs alongside the Thames River, with beach chairs one could rent for 36 pence per hour. We stopped for a while, realized that we had walked a long way. Shortly after our rest we found the school building.

The first school day was a scary situation for me. I worried if I could keep up, or if my school mate would be too far ahead of me. First of all we, Renate and I, got to the first class ½ hour late. It took time to find the street the school was on. Then we were delayed in the school office to get our books. The first hour of school was already in full swing. The school was in an old building, or maybe it had been a warehouse at one time. The rooms were small, the classes were partitioned off.

I got put in with Renate, Erika, Hella, the blond Claudia and a fat little girl named Marion. She was placed with Erika, from Berlin, in one family. Erika and I had the same destination in Scotland, once we were done here in London. Of all of them, I was the least knowledgeable and understood next to nothing. After two sentences I had enough, I could not understand a word. I stopped participating and wrote down the vocabulary that was given instead. Those we were to learn for the next day.

Then I began to study my classmates. I was bored, due to not being able to follow the lessons. This was a risk and I knew it; my English was just not good enough. I had to get with it, in a big way. It was not that I did not want to, or that I was lazy. I was not. I just was not up to speed, like the others, I just did not have enough English preparation under my belt. But it would come, I was convinced, just when, I was not sure.

The classes were from advanced English to hardly enough like me. Intelligence was also in all directions, some very smart or clever, other arrogant, or too simple. What they believed in I had still to find out. Wonder why that was important to me? I hoped that I would be able to find out, sooner or later. I knew, I could tell that those that took credit for having had English, tried to follow the class lessons, but there were still plenty that had only meager knowledge. I told myself that with everything, there had to be a beginning. I had taken my first step.

I was here, I was in the right environment. I was thinking that after 6 to 8 years of school English, I would have thought, all would have more practice. That made me think, I would be OK. Classes from 9:30 to 12.30 pm, small break and food in cafeteria.

The coffee was awful and tasted like the German *Muckefuck*. Some kind of concoction that was sold as coffee, after the war. It was not, coffee that is, just tasted like it, but then, not really. *"Lindes ja der schmeckt"* a slogan in Germany, that advertised this concoction. I had tea, from then on at 30 pence per cup. After our first school day we went to Victoria Train Station to retrieve our suitcases. They had arrived from the border. After taking care of the paperwork, we took the suitcases and went home, but not before we managed to secure a porter who took our suitcases straight to where we lived. It was difficult to travel with suitcases. Buses and trains only stopped a split second, if you were not ready to jump out, with your belongings, you would miss your stop, or you got separated from your stuff. So you had to be prepared to be ready with sack and pack, to jump out.

The porter did not leave until he had secured the adequate tip, we found out. The trains were small, with large sofas, like in grandmother's living room. As I found out later, they just went in between the little towns.

That very night we, Renate and I went to the cinema in which one could smoke if one wanted too. It was open all day, one could stay in it all day long. Renate had a cousin that studied economics here in London. We made a date for next Wednesday. Our second day in London would entail a city tour conducted by the school.

I was right; it is difficult to get to school on time from our living quarters. I am glad that as of the second week, we could actually walk to it, what a relief! The bus or the subway would have taken up too much of my money. That would have been my biggest expense. This week it cost me *3 Deutsch Marks,* before exchange.

The city tour was good, the teacher spoke only English, but it did not matter, because it gave us a very good orientation through London, along Big Ben, Westminister Abbey, Parliament, St. James Park, and Hyde Park to St. Paul Cathedral. This is the seat of the bishop of London. That was a wonderful building. Here also were famous British personalities buried. The clocks in Big Ben are supposed to weigh 17 ton.

Then towards the Tower Bridge and further on to the Tower of London. In the middle ages it was a palace, later a state prison where gruesome tortures happened. We saw the block were they chopped off heads. Three queens died here on it (decapitated) and lots of people guilty or not, so they say, who got in the way of the ruling class, kings, queens, statesmen and clergy, alike.

These walls still gave out a sinister impression. More so since it had just started to rain, the day gray and unfriendly. In this tower we saw the crown jewels, weapons, swords, spears, knight's suits and a great medieval collection. A colorful guard stood watch in front of the tower, just like in front of the Buckingham Palace; in their colorful costumes to watch over all of it. They stood there today, just like they did hundreds of years ago.

After that we went to the National Gallery, Piccadilly Circus, Trafalgar Square with the statue of Nelson, on to the house guard of the queen, to Buckingham Palace, then to the changing of the guard.

After that, we went sight seeing every day straight after classes from 2 pm to 10 pm, by foot, by subway, by bus. We went riding and boating in Hyde Park, we listened to all these people speaking in Hyde Park, exercising their right to free speech, about God knows what. They expressed their views on politics and economics. Here they could talk freely or wore shields, on which they expressed their views. Even when they railed against their own Government nobody paid attention. The bobbies were there in great number, no guns on them, to keep peace or separate the ruffians from each other. We went several times to see the changing of the guards at the Buckingham Palace. We went to most of the Museums, we went to the Planetarium to listen about the stars, we went to Madame Tussauds Exhibition, Wax museum. I got separated from the girls there, I stopped to ask a policeman, who stood in the hallway for directions,

then I had to see to my utter embarrassment, that I was talking to a wax figure. Boy, he was so lifelike, only when he did not answer me, I took a closer look and I saw my mistake. We saw President Kennedy there in Wax and lots more.

On Sundays we went to Petticoat Lane Market, the biggest open market I had ever seen, where you could buy just about anything, new or old. I was reminded of the flea market in Paris.

We went to look at the big department stores alongside the Thames, we got lost in Soho, with those tiny little streets through it. This was the part of town where the underworld hung out. It gave us a shudder feeling, to wander through it, especially at night.

Somewhere in that time frame, I absolutely could no longer walk anymore in my nice shoes with heels. One day, while sightseeing, I came across a shoe store that had sneakers. Good Lord, sneakers my first pair, what a good thing it was. My feet were saved, I never wore anything else from that time on, except when we went out dancing. Actually, I took my high heels in a bag, to put on when I got to the dance hall.

We went to a Shakespeare festival that was being conducted, but only went to the free stuff, no money for the evening shows. So for six weeks we were all over London. When we got back at night, Mrs. B was waiting for us, with a full dinner. She would not leave our sight, until we ate all she prepared.

But I still could not understand what she told me, Renate had to translate for me later. Whenever we came back from an outing, she had more points of interest for us, which we just absolutely had to see.

She was also the one to fill us in about the dance places to go to. Renate would not, but Erika and I went whenever we had some steam left. We just had to make sure to catch the last train, subway or bus, before 1 pm, or we would be stuck and had no way to get back, besides walking. We got picked up by a police patrol, once. They took us home. pretty decent of them!

Now let me explain the dance places. Most had entry fees that were too expensive, but we found a few that fitted our budget. We picked the Lucano. When we arrived, we saw hundreds of young people, between the ages of 16 to 22. The Lucano had a big dance floor, which could handle about 100 couples. Somewhere on the second level there was another smaller dance floor, around lots of tables, little niches, balconies with a good view of what was going on. Four different bars alongside the walls. The second floor also had several bars alongside the walls. One could get all kinds of drinks, including milk. Nobody was forced to order, you got it yourself. The dancers, or those wanting to dance, hung around the dance floor, viewing potential partners, hoping for a sign.

When you got a drink from the bars and had secured a table, then went dancing, your table was gone, your seat too. You left it, you lost it, no matter if your glass was still on the table. So, either you sit or you stood around or danced. Did not matter if you had your coat hanging on the chair it was gone nonetheless. Everybody could sit on whatever chair was free.

191

After a while we got the drift of this method. There was a place where you could leave your coat and your purse, which you retrieved again when you left or had to use the toilet. The dance was different. It looked funny and was difficult to dance too. Then the girls, some of them danced with each other, instead of men. I even saw several men dancing together, whatever that was about. The dance was a cross between twist and something that had not arrived in Germany yet. I most certainly had not seen it, I was thinking.

It was then that I felt a hand on my shoulder; it took me by surprise. I turned around to look at the person who touched me; it sent a strange sensation down my spine. I was staring at a uniform. He was tall, this man, he still had not removed his hand from my shoulder, however the pressure was soft and light. I found it daring, just the same. I looked him up and down; he made a smashing figure in that uniform.

I found his eyes, dancing all over my face, smiling, asking me for a dance. Of course that is what he wants, why else is he hanging around here? I liked the uniform and this man in it. He guided me onto the dance floor, still he had his hand on my shoulder, with all that pushing and shuffling around us, I guess he did not want to lose me in the crowd. I had nodded in agreement, went ahead of him onto the floor, hoping he would not remove his hand from my shoulder. He did, but immediately placed it around my hips. Never had I found anybody's touch so unsettling and nice at the same time. It was dark and I was glad about it, he could not see my face. I might have sprouted a rose color, hence giving myself away.

He was quite tall and looked very handsome in his uniform. I did not recognize it. It could not be English, could it? When he started to make conversation with me, I knew right a way, he was American. Of all the guys here, I had to be asked by an American soldier to dance. His English sounded a lot different.

His voice was a soft growl and he was showering me with questions. Finally he held me firmly at arms length, a broad smile covered his whole face. He had figured out that I had not understood one single word he said to me. All this time he held me in a firm grip, just barely, keeping the social bearing intact. I tried to get mine back, I even managed a smile.

I told him my name is "Rosemarie, I am German, and speak little English."

He would only let go of me a little bit, maybe he felt I was a bit uncomfortable, yet he never let go of me all together. However, he did not once overstep the boundaries. The music was now changing into swing. I found myself willing to get into it. I was going to enjoy this nice dance partner. I moved a bit closer, now and then, feeling his body next to mine. What was so different about him, what did this mean, here in this strange city?

His name was Fred, I found out when Erika interrogated him a bit later, herself having found a dance partner, Eddie by name, who could have been the spitting image of Sammy Davis Jr., except for his eyes. I found out that Fred was on a military TDY, meaning "travel during the year" until next Monday, visiting in London. He was stationed in Germany, of all places.

We danced all night, we exchanged addresses. We danced close, held hands, I had great trouble keeping a distance between us. We went for smoke breaks, we kissed, ever so lightly, he kissed me, I did not object. As the evening went on, he offered to take us home, by car; his buddies had a car.

We had discovered them among the dancers; they were all in uniform. We made a date for the next day, because by Monday he would be back in Germany. He invited us to visit him and his buddies on the American ship in the harbor. He was staying there, while on TDY. He was not in the Navy, he was in the Air Force in

Ramstein, Germany. I did not sleep much that night, thinking about him, I liked him a lot. What was so special about his touch? I could not understand it. I did not have time to fall in love, I thought, it does not fit into my plans.

So the next day, Sunday, we went to visit. It was quite a task to get ourselves down to the harbor, but as soon as we made it, we could not miss the only American ship in the harbor. It seemed the entire crew took us on a tour of the ship. Fred could not get rid of them, it was fun, so much attention. When we disembarked the whole of the ship was lined by sailors waving good bye to us. I left wondering would I ever see him again?

Our days were filled with learning, sightseeing and getting used to the English way of life. Erika had by now a regular dating situation going on with Sammy Jr., the nick name for Eddie. Now I don't even remember his real name. We just called him Sammy Davis Jr., instead Eddie, when we referred to him. Often I was invited, as well. School in the day time, dancing on the week ends, there was not much time to think about Fred, our time here was almost over.

When we danced at the Lugano, Erika met Eddie there, while I had to content myself dancing with who ever asked me. Around midnight we would stop because we had to rush to the bus station, to make sure we got home. After 1 pm nothing was moving, when it had to do with city transportation. Eddie took great interest in Erika and since he was very familiar with London, he had been showing us around, but constantly tried to set me up with one of his friends, also a student. Eddie was very generous and since I tagged along, he always invited me and paid my bill, as well. He was American and had money.

The last Friday he picked us up from the subway and dragged us through the university, through all cafes, we finally landed in Soho around 6 pm. There we waited for a friend, whom he had invited to come; we were to go out us a foursome. Boy, I did not feel very happy about that. A blind date, no less. His friend, a student also, showed up and he looked like straight out of the bush. All he needed was a bone through his hair. His name was Ashbarhorse and he was so black, you would only see the white of his teeth, now that it was dark. He really looked like a tribal man, somewhere out of the deep of Africa. His head was sort of a melon form, his hair was really stripy, thick, an Afro, he had those big fat lips, that could have sported a ring as well, just like in the movies, just like certain tribes in Africa. He was only the second black man I had ever met, next to Eddie, who was Erika's friend.

Well, that was Ashbarhorse, that was how he looked from the outside. Otherwise he was extremely well taken care of, refined. He told me he was the son of a tribal chief, in Africa, studied here in London. He made a good first impression, if I could have been able to get over the way he looked. After Sammy introduced him, he reached for my hand, I knew it, boy oh boy, he thinks we are on a date. Blind date, but a date nonetheless. I was not too happy about that.

I had no knowledge in how to proceed to keep this fellow off me. Not letting him think that I was interested and at the same time trying not to hurt his feelings. I had no experience on how to deal with a tribal chief's, son. First they took us to a fast food shop, we ate, had two whiskys and palavered on where to go. They decided to go to the Flamingo club of which both were members. I was knee deep in Soho with two guys, on a date, I had not organized myself. I had no way of getting out of it, since I had no way to get home.

Erika seemed to trust her Sammy Jr., (Eddie) and found nothing wrong with Ashbarhorse being my blind date. I could hardly stop thinking about how many things could go wrong with this scenario. Just plain go wrong. There were a lot of black young men around here, I thought, most of them were students. Most of them were here with white girls, dancing up a storm. In Germany I had not seen many blacks, I never knew one or dated one. I felt uncomfortable.

Erika seemed to prefer them, at least her Sammy Davis Jr. look a like. She trusted him. What was I to do now, anyway. It was 1963, the races still did not mix too often, in Germany. London was different, here at the Flamingo Club it was very apparent. So I danced with my tribal chief's son, at least I tried to dance. Again this silly dance routine, which I had never seen before. Now I found out what the dance was. It was called the Shake. One would stand or slightly move, shake everything, including body parts. We stayed a while then changed over to a different dance hall.

By the end of the night the boys wanted to continue the party in their apartment and Erika argued with me that we were to four, it would be OK. I did not like it, but I had no way of going home by myself. I did not even know where we were. We went to their student housing, their room was in ruins, like a disaster area, I was shocked. They had however a really big TV and several bottles of whisky, which I did not partake in.

As soon as we started dancing Erika and Sammy Jr. took a powder. I was left with Ashbar, now I was calling him that, because his name was just to long to remember. Also I did not know, was the end of his name really "Horse?" I was not sure and did not want make a mistake.

It took some thinking and maneuvering to keep Ashbarhorse off my person, he wanted to be romantic. I had to think on my feet and used all kind of methods to keep him from being too romantic. He actually told me that in his homeland he could have more then one wife. Good Grief, what was he trying to say? He was no different than other young men of his age, I realized this right away. I could tell he liked me and I tried not to be harsh, but "really," did I get that right, with his being able to have four wives? "Well, not in my life time." So I started my palaver to keep him off me and tried not to be to stern with him.

I did not want to make him angry. Boy, oh Boy what a bad situation had Erika got me into. Even with a boy that I found charming I would not have proceeded to be in a World City, alone, in Soho, the underworld meeting place. How stupid of an idea was this to begin with. Still we made conversation and somehow I got the gist of what he meant. He spoke good English.

I am writing this, after I got home safe, but I was sweating bullets all the way home, until the door closed behind me and I was inside the house. While Erika went off outside, or out of my view, Ashbarhorse and I waited for the driver, again friend of theirs, who had a VW, to come at midnight, to bring us all home.

Two friends came so four of us had to pile into the back of the VW. It was the middle of the night. Erika could not really remember what direction we had to go, for home. Her to her place, I to mine. We went all over London in the approximate direction, that we suspected we lived in. Erika finally was able to deliver her address, so of course they took her home first, because that is what she remembered.

Now I was stuck in the car with four strangers, black men, at that, all of them students. I started to pray in earnest, because I feared that this was it. I was sure I was going to be found somewhere dead. Meanwhile, we had figured out where I lived, it took another 15 minutes to get me there.

197

I suppose that they felt my uneasiness because they insisted that they bring me to my front door and wait outside, until I closed the door behind me. I gathered from the last conversation, or at least part of it, that they had to make sure that I got home safe. I was with them, so they had to make sure they could not just set me up on my street, as I had suggested, they had to make sure, that I was safely inside my home. I just wanted to get out of that damn car.

Well, I lucked out. They were decent boys, not stupid either and they made sure that I was safely delivered home, with them all witnessing that I went inside, the door closed behind me. Then they took off. Thank God. I was going to give Erika a few choice words. Another lesson. Do not trust any arrangement, other than one made by yourself. The six weeks are over and tomorrow we go by train to Rhu in West Scotland.

Chapter 32

Scotland

May 1963 we are on our way to Rhu in West Scotland. We met 9:30 am at Eusten Station. My suitcases had already gone two days ago and we would pick them up at the station in Rhu. We were going by train. Actually the suitcases were supposed to be delivered directly to where we were staying. I hoped that was the case. I  worried because here in England things did not happen in the same dependable way as in Germany.

We would go by train from Eusten direct to Glasgow. Then by bus to Rhu-Helensburgh which was a little tourist town and the address of the youth hostel. They had a café restaurant car on the train, lots of pretty country to look at, while the engine was steaming through it. Soon we had male company. It did not seem to be difficult here; they just showed up, started a conversation, or we, that is Erika did.

Here I found out that the English word for kiss is suppose to be "yum yum." Not true, I think, it was something altogether different. I figured that out later, much later. We were having fun with "yum yum" all the way to Glasgow. Actually it made sense when one thinks about it. Yummy is tasty or delightful. Not bad to describe a kiss.

We found ways to make small talk with other passengers on the train as well and soon found a lady that had the same destination, Rhu. She offered us a ride in her car. Her sister was to pick her up in Glasgow. That was very agreeable, since it was already a long ride and it saved us changing trains in Glasgow, then the bus to Helensburgh. People were so friendly here in England, much more than in Germany.

I remember some would actually cross the street rather than give you directions, that is in Germany, not here. My friend Edelgard, for instance, who pretended not to speak English in the street car, when someone asked for directions. I questioned her on that but she just shrugged her shoulders, told me she did not talk to foreigners. This is the first time that I became aware of the German way being different, which sometimes means not being friendly at all. I liked this way better.

This lady we have been talking with told us about herself and her sister. They live together. Both sisters were never married. Her age must have been around 60. I also noted that England had a lot of old people, everywhere. "How come I did not notice that many old people in Germany?" I am sure we had them, we must have old people. They could not been killed off in the war. At least not all of them. But here they were also working still, older people, like in their 60s. Never noticed that in Germany.

Her sister came with a dog, that she had just found, it smelled something terrible. There was no time yet to give it a bath, to clean it up. It was a street dog, she did not know who it belonged to. All English people are extremely fond of animals, does not matter what, dogs, cats and birds, she told us. So we crammed into her VW. Erika, the two ladies, myself, the dog all crammed into the VW and off to Helensburgh, we went. They delivered us directly to the front door of the youth hostel.

Helenburgh is the shopping center for people living in Rhu we were told, and it was directly on a lake. The main street went alongside the lake. I wondered if this was one of the famous Lochs? This one was named Loch Garre. It seems all the lakes here are called Lochs. I remember reading about the Loch Ness monster. But this was not that Loch. I went to that one later on, but did not see the monster. Loch in German means hole! So they called their lakes Lochs!

There were several different yard harbors with lots of boats. It was pretty here, very isolated, lots of green woods, lonely places, hills around in the distance and the moor. No, it was more like a moat and one could get stuck in it, if one was not careful. This is because of the rain. It rained here ever day; you would not go out without your umbrella, ever.

We got to our new home "At Ardenconnel" at 6 pm that night. This house used to be a feudal residence. The entire front and especially the inside spoke of a great residence, of a long past feudal history. The stairs in front of the house brought you to a front door that was huge, with an entry key six to eight inches long, which the First Lady would lock each night, at 11 pm. Nobody in or out without her knowledge. I found out later.

Inside, large stairs led up or down or around to different parts of the house. Most were built into guest rooms, even some in the basement, where the staff rooms were, lounge for the staff, the eating area, the kitchen, the wash rooms.

Right inside the front door was a huge lobby, from which all kinds of rooms went in all directions. There was a staircase going up into the 2nd floor and 3rd floor or down into the basement. Right here on the

1st floor we found the guest lounge with fireplace, the playroom with intercom, phone, tennis table and in both rooms a big piano.

The view from the guest lounge and playroom was going out over to the lake (Loch). Then came the very large dining room and the little dining room, the writing room with fireplace, the offices of the first lady and of the male secretary. Those were downstairs facing the garden. The secretary, the only male staff person, except for *"Rumpelstiltskin"* also faced the garden, Their view was very green, wet and pretty but always wet. Scotland has a lot of rain.

On this level we also had six guest rooms; I was scheduled to take care of them. In the basement we had two dish wash kitchen, one for the big dining room, one for the little dining room. Then there was a linen closet for towels and linen. This room was always very hot and humid, because the hot water boilers were close by in the basement.

The linen room was used by us to dry our clothes. We were not supposed to, but the boss ladies chose to ignore it. We had to dry our clothes somewhere, outside was not possible, because of the constant rain. The basement had the kitchen, the cake room or sandwich rooms, where we had to assemble lunch packs to give to the guests for their day trips.

Then, there was the dining room of the staff, two toilets, three guest bath rooms, showers and three more guests rooms, plus lots more little corridors, niches and unused rooms. The linen room had also an ironing board with an iron, which I promptly dropped the first week I was there. It never really worked after that treatment. The rooms did not have bathrooms, toilet, or showers. They were on the same floor, shared, but not in each room.

Next to the entry hall all rooms were guest rooms. On the first floor were the bedrooms of the bosses, the first lady, second, the cook, plus bath, shower and toilets. It also had a bunch of guest rooms. On the 2nd and 3rd floor were more guest rooms plus we, the au pairs had our room. Erika, Susan and I shared one room. It overlooked the backside of the house and the garden. We could see the little garden house, a small ways off, which housed the *"Rumpelstiltskin,"* the secretary and any unattached males, meaning not married. We called the cottage the "bachelor pad."

Behind that garden house and the bachelor's pad, was the crematorium. We called it such, because it was a built out fire pit, where whatever was able to burn, would be burned. A little wild creek separated our house and ground from the next property. It was difficult to cross, because one would get stuck in the marshland, along side the creek. I tried, but had to abandon it, after sinking to my ankles into the mud, having trouble to get back out.

Well, we got there at 6 pm and were greeted by the 1st and 2nd lady. The 1st Lady was the boss and quite a bit younger then the 2nd lady, who was in charge of the operation, each day, and work allotment. The 2nd lady was about 60 years, little, very fast on her feet, all over the place. She came up behind us in all kinds of situations, when we least expected her.

The 2nd lady called a girl by the name of Susan, a girl from Switzerland, here for the same reason as I. She was 22 years old, just like myself, slender and skinny. She was happy to see us. Now she was no longer alone, struggling barely speaking English. The German she spoke, with a Swiss accent, was kind of endearing. Our room number was 26 on the 3rd floor.

We freshened up and were told dinner was to be at 6:30 pm, like every week day. Soon after we noticed a loud whistle sound, which was the call for dinner. It sounded just like a policeman's whistle. It turned out to be a whistle alright. It was the cook who blew it, that was her job. It was used to call the staff to lunch, dinner, tea and to breakfast. Not the guests, just the staff. Susan told us to go to the staff dining room whenever we heard it, promptly.

We went and met the cook, the other staff members, plus the secretary we nicknamed "the sexy-terry" because he was the only male young enough, to matter, to us at all. He was early 20s very slender and very English looking, whatever that means. Nobody thought he was very attractive but he was the only game in town.

Most of the women were older, if not to say really old. There was one young girl by the name of Joan, who came from somewhere in Scotland. She was fat, dressed very unfortunately for her size. When she laughed you could see that all her teeth were black. She did not seem to have one healthy tooth in her mouth. I wondered if that was the great amount of sweets that the English liked so much.

We, the au pairs, sat at the end of the table, which held twelve people. The only man was Mister Johnson. Again a very old, little man, small wrinkled and not very clean. At least he looked that way, not very appetizing. He was the man for all odd jobs. He was the jack of all trades, whatever needed done, he was called on. He also was supposed to do the dishes.

We gave him the name of *"Rumpelstiltskin,"* like in the German fairy tale. He kind of looked like it, very small, almost like a gnome, big nose, fat lips, a small frame and bony hands. He walked a bit bent over and of course he was old, I think very old.

First a soup was served, which was an extremely important procedure and only the 1st lady could serve it. It was her job and felt like a ceremony. It had to be the correct way, done by a higher staff member. That was for the soup only. The rest of the food distribution had to be done by us, taking turns.

Every day, two different girls were picked to serve the others. In between we were also able to eat. After dinner we, whose turn it was, had to clear the table and bring the dishes into the dish wash kitchen. After the soup was served by the first lady, she spoke a brief prayer and we were able to eat, starting now with the main dish.

Today it was turkey (eaten here often, also lamb) potatoes, stuffing (had no idea what that was), soup and apple sauce, cauliflowers as veggie. Then there was dessert, always dessert. Today it was some kind of vanilla pudding with a piece of cake swimming in it. Tasted good. After that we would be offered tea. The entire event would take about 45 minutes.

After dinner all the other staff members went off to their assigned jobs which they got from the 2nd lady. In about 5 minutes the whistle sounded again. All staff, except the two new ones, us, went up to the big dining room to serve the guests their dinner. Susan was given the night off to get us settled and show us around. The workday would start for us tomorrow.

Chapter 33

Ardenconnel, Rhu, (Scotland)

At precisely 8 am each morning an alarm bell went off and was heard through the house on every floor. It sounded like a fire alarm, or like a school bell, when break was over. That is how the guests were awakened each morning. For us it was the sign to show up to do breakfast before the guests got ready for theirs. Then when we were ready, or that is to say, when the guests food was ready, one of us went through the hallways with a big bell making enough noise for

the dead to wake up, which told the guests to assemble in front of the dining room. Each day it was the same, except with another girl to ring the bell, calling the guests, for whatever time we were serving. Everything was so different, so interesting, I knew I was going to have great fun.

Susan was given the task of supervising our first assignments, how fast we were to work, and by what method. That was extremely important. She explained if we were too fast or too good, we would have to pick up the slack of the others. In general, we needed to slow a bit, not to be faster then the older ladies, who could not work fast. Besides it seemed to be considered bad form, disrespectful toward the older folks, meaning the 50 plus crowd of the employees. There were definitely a few of those around.

Monday morning was my first day of work. It started at 7:30 am and we were assigned the work before breakfast was ready. We took a cup of tea, wherever we started our duties. I was assigned to clean the fireplace in the writing room and to fill it up with new charcoal briquettes. I was to do it the same way, exactly, not to invent a better way, but just go by the method she told us. All work had to follow a certain method exactly, as we were shown how to do it, after long years of tradition. It felt like the upstairs downstairs series, that I was to watch on TV years later. After that I got the broom, the mop and went on dusting. By 8 am, the "breakfast" whistle did not go off, but Mrs. Duffy, the cook went by wherever we were assigned and gathered us up for breakfast. We hurried down for breakfast. I was always ready to eat. It was always held in the same room, same time, with the work assignments waiting for each of us afterward.

Can't say too much about Mrs. Duffy. She was small, a great cook and baker, but very quiet, said nothing most of the time and she had a 15 year old son. Well, she could not have been that old. Not if she had a 15 year old son. The only thing I found noteworthy is that she sprouted a nicely powdered rose red nose. Nobody knows why she was here and not with her husband and son.

As soon as we got to the staff room our jobs were assigned by Mrs. Mc Nickels (from now on Mrs. Mick Mack) to service the staff first. Mrs. Mick Mack was Scottish, with a sing song kind of a voice. She was loud, aggressive and knew everything better than anybody. She knew everything and did everything better, but never was seen doing it herself. She was mostly gone when it came to real work. We could not ever find her when we needed her to be assigned, or complete her jobs. After a while we got wise and found her in the breakfast room, making sandwiches for the day tours that all the guests were taking all over the country side. She also was the better part of 60

years old, maybe even more.

The most original, Mrs. Diament, was 42 years old, just ran away from her husband. She left him, she told us. She has a 15 year old daughter and a dog. When she is not singing she is crying about not seeing her dog. She misses him. She smokes like a chimney and goes into one of the toilets to smoke. She is sprouting a very ill fitted set of false teeth that give her a lot of problems when she eats. We keep watching her at lunch or at dinner, when she routinely loses her teeth, they drop down, to our great amusement. We are still a bunch of teenagers, howling at everything that its different from us. However, she is always in a good mood and is responsible for a good portion of our entertainment here.

Breakfast consisted of prunes, cornflakes or porridge, toast (brown or white bread) marmalade and one fried egg on a piece of raw bacon. This particular day, while we were still eating, Susan went off to ring the bell. The order would go out "ring the bell" and one of us would jump up, go up and down the hallways, to let the guests know that now they could assemble for their breakfast. It was fun to run the bell through the entire house we could hear the sound of it going further and further away, into the belly of the house, and all the different floors.

Breakfast took 45 minutes and after that the dishes were loaded up onto a trolley, taken to the kitchen, where it would be Mr. Johnson's job to wash them. One of us was to dry them. However, most of the time we left "Rumpelstiltskin" alone. Did I mention before we called him that because he was little, and truly looked like a gnome. He reminded us of a character in a German fairy tale.

The whistle went off. We were all going to get breakfast for the guests going in the big dining room, which was upstairs and we had to use the dumb waiter. Never seen one of these before. It was a lift that was used to bring the plates and food to the big dining room on the next floor. It was a box in the wall and operated with a thick rope which had to be pulled from downstairs. The next person pulled it up from the dining room. Sometimes we put too much in it. When one or the other person did not have a good grip it went crashing down again, broke all the dishes in it.

Usually it got to come up half way, then we could not hold on to it any longer, it went crashing down, with a great deal of noise, got everybody running to see, to make sure none of us had their hand in it or their head, while trying to see how far up it was. It was a dangerous undertaking. We all knew about it and made sure none of our vital parts were anywhere in the part of the dumb waiter crashing down. I had to let go of it several times and it went crashing down, before we the au pairs, came to an understanding how much could be loaded into it.

By 9 am one of us would be sent to ring the breakfast bell for the guests, after we had set the table for them. All of us jumped at it because we all like to run through the hallways, to ring the bell, to make as much noise at the bell would give off. By that time most the guests had already assembled themselves in the lounge, or stood hungry in front of the dining room, asking whoever went by "are you going to ring the bell?" When the answer was "Yes" they pushed closer to the still closed door, to get to their assigned places once the door was open and the bell was heard. It was like this every day, day in and day out, every week, simply always. There was a routine and it was never changed. Everybody knew the rules.

There were always appetizers, main course und dessert. The guests had one hour to eat. In between, we started to wash up what was empty. Mostly us three. The Swiss Susan, Erika from Berlin, and I from Duesseldorf, *"the 3 musketeers,"* or au pairs.

Nobody really wanted to dry dishes and washing dishes was frowned on by the staff. We just got it done. If the 2nd lady found any of the staff without work, she would send them to wash up, but never knew when they just disappeared.

We dragged the washing of dishes out as long as we could, because we wanted to make sure not to miss the postman, in his little red car. If we were finished too early, we would go to our assigned jobs, had to wait for the mail call, in the afternoon. We wanted it sooner, so we devised some kind of way for one of us to be close, so we could receive the mail and pass it on before the afternoon. It seemed to be the only connection with the out-side world and sometimes we got little boxes and we shared them. I didn't think people at home thought we didn't get enough to eat. It was mostly fun stuff and new clothes. On Sundays there was no mail. But we would try to guess who would get mail or a box and we took bets on who would get the most mail.

My first work assignment was with Mrs. Smith and we had to do six rooms. Today we would call this hospitality crew. Mrs. Smith told me that she had seen better days, had fallen on hard times and now in her old age she still had to take on a summer job. She was 70 years old, of ill health and terribly sensitive. She had a nervous tic around her mouth and would babble to herself, sometimes I found her staring into the air. I felt sorry for her and did her work, also. She did not like that, she could not understand that I wanted to help her, because she seemed so frail. She balled me out, told me she could do her own work, which was assigned to her.

After a while I was told by the 2nd lady, who took me into the sandwich room, that she would give me the six rooms to work by myself. The first week, in which I still worked with Mrs. Smith, went so slow I thought I would fall asleep standing up. She was very slow. But off course I was so much younger and had a lot of energy. She also complained to the 2nd lady that I was working too fast. This was the reason that I got the six rooms by myself. However while the first week was coming to end the 2nd lady told me not to work faster then Mrs. Smith. I was always finished first, showed up for more work, which set these English ladies into an uproar.

Chapter 34

The First Week and Beyond

The first week has gone by, I still don't understand much, which resulted in making up the wrong beds, or fetching the wrong item. Instead of the vacuum cleaner I get the broom. Another time, it was my turn to be the water and bread girl. I ask the first lady a question, she thought I was complaining. It took somebody else to translate. I was not, just asking a question. She did not understand either. Lots of exasperation palaver, to get it right. I had just asked a question. Then I got a cold, did not feel like eating supper, which made everybody show up at my bedside to inquire what was wrong with me and how could they help me.

We had a fair turnover of staff. It seemed they were always coming and going. The guests themselves only stayed one week. Therefore we had to deal with different people every week. No idea why. They became unhappy and just left. This place had an older population of guests, I would say over 50, very stiff in their behavior. Some actually not too pleased to see young Germans, here on the staff. The war was still hanging in the air, for them.

In week three was a turnover again; several left and two new ones showed up. I was still working too fast, that is when I decided to continue with my journal. I would finish my rooms, then I took the rest of the time to record what had happened previously. I had bought a steno block last week on my day off. It would keep me from getting into trouble when I finished too fast. We were not to show up the elder ladies, not that we, or I did it on purpose. They worked so slow that I could fall asleep standing up watching them. I just could not do it. I actually had bought yarn; Susan was going to

 show me how to knit a sweater, plus a beanie. Whenever I showed up at the 2nd lady's office to tell her "I am finished," I got bad looks from the rest, not from the au pairs, but the locals.

It was told that it was unkind for the rest of the eldery staff, like Mrs. Smith, that the young girls would finish so fast and always ahead of the rest of the staff. I would embarrass them; I just needed to slow down. Well problem solved, I just stayed in the room the extra time, keeping records of whatever had happened that day.

So what was my job? I had six bedrooms and made the beds, cleaned the sink, each room had one, then vacuum, or mop it and empty the paper baskets. On the floor was a female bathroom, a male bathroom and one shower. I did not need three hours for that work especially not since I had to work per English example, shown me not only in the beginning, but every day anew, we received exact instructions.

It would change on Sunday, when we had a half hour less time, because everybody slept longer. That day we did not clean, just made the beds and emptied the waste paper baskets. Then again on Thursday, we really gave every room just a "Lick and a Promise," because that was the day, by instruction of the ladies, that we had to wax the bathroom floors.

Boy, once I was caught wet washing the floor first, before waxing. I got in a lot of trouble. That only happened by direct management orders. Nothing, absolutely, nothing was done without detailed instruction, per tradition. After that incident, I thought, I was practically forced to push the dust from one corner of the bedroom into the other corner. Really, that was the gist of it. Can't understand why I could not do it the right way, the German way.

On Saturday we would get a new batch of guests, and then we had to put new linen on the beds. That in itself was an ordeal, since it was to be done exactly as instructed and on occasion somebody would inspect us. Also, there were no feather beds, no down; only blankets, but one could have as many as one needed, to keep warm. Then on Saturdays, we doubled up to make the rooms, it was easier to make the beds. On the new guest day all regular work was not done either. The old Mrs. Smith was the one that showed me how to do the beds. She is the one that complained about me, because I was too fast. On Saturday and Sunday the guests stayed in, no tour anywhere.

At 4 pm was High Tea, always a very big affair, cakes, breads, cucumber sandwiches, sweets of all kinds and entertainment before and after. There were games in the playroom, table tennis, card games, piano concerts, put on by the guests on Sundays and the male guests were to serve the ladies. That was fun to watch. They walked around with the cups of tea, the plates of cakes; everybody could take as much as they could eat. By the end, the male guests had to take the plates and cups downstairs and wash the dishes, which was conducted with great fan fare and laughter. It surprised me that the English, in fact, had a sense of humor; so far it had eluded me. They were so stiff, tradition minded, but not on the game nights and when they served the ladies. Actually we, the girls, had wondered about how these English people procreated. It seemed to us that there was absolutely no show of affection. Well, I was wrong on that account. They just kept it under wraps, the ones that were somewhat upper class, anyway. We just put the clean dishes into the cupboard.

215

In general I ate too much, too many goodies were offered. I was nearly unable to consume the supper, afterward. Fortunately supper on Sundays was mostly salad leave, tomatoes, red beets, plus cheese and cookies.

Then there was a kind of a service, somebody read out of the Bible. The guests sang, then they played more cards, some would sing songs or recite poems. Then the secretary "our only male staff member" showed *"dias"* a slide show of areas that could be visited on the day trips. So it went every Sunday, and by midnight the house was quiet, all the doors closed and the 1ˢᵗ lady had locked the front door with this super big key, which was kept in her room. By 7 am, the next morning, the door would be unlocked by her again.

Mrs. Diament will leave us by the end of the week. She will go back to her husband and her dog that she had been whining about for weeks. We would get somebody new, hopefully somebody younger. In all respects we liked it here, even when the habits were so different at times. The other day Mrs. Diament was out of dish soap, she went into the washroom, got a piece of soap, *"Kernseife"* curd-soap, ran it over the washcloth several times, to soap it up, and here we go, she was washing the dishes that way, always with such speed that the water was splashing all over her and the kitchen. She always worked with great speed. If we knew she had dish wash duties we would inspect our silver closely.

Every day the guests would greet us "Nice day, isn't?" or we would be asked "Do you like England?" Every week we would have to explain where we came from and what our deal was. We got used to the Scottish dances at night, the men in skirts, the music they played, and we went on the day tours with the guests on our free days. I saw a lot of country that way. A lot of Lochs and a lot of castles.

I stopped trying to change them to clean the German way. I just no longer paid attention and stayed out of their way. We had long midday breaks, in which we played with the many stray cats; we knitted, we went to visit the ladies with the dog, who had first delivered us there. We went hiking around the Lochs (lakes) and discovered "Dr. Kildare" on TV, which I got addicted to. I wrote several letters to Fred and had no answer yet: "had he forgotten about me?" He told me it took longer, the letters had a "AP" army post address; went to a general military collection spot, from there they would be send to wherever the guys were stationed.

We always had a long break after lunch, because all were gone on tours. There was no entertainment, no movie center. The "pub" tavern was closed at 10 pm and one could not enter unless we were accompanied by a man. Hence the *"sexy-terry,"* the only available male, was enlisted once in a while to get us in. But that was boring also.

We lost more ladies, Mrs. Mick-Mack, Mrs. Smith and the Diamond woman, they were gone now. Replacement was Hip, a very young girl, she would have received the "Nobel Price" for laziness, had there been one. She only lasted one week. She was let go.

After that Carol showed up. Carol was 16 years old. She was a typical teenager and introduced us on her 2nd day to her Scottish boyfriend, whom she claimed she would marry before she went home. She was a great new distraction because not one day would go by without her doing something outrageous, or stupid. Most days she showed up too late for work. She went out at night, did not come back in time, so the door was locked and she had to alarm the 1st lady to get into the house. She overslept, came to her duties late, or did not show up at all, because she was out with lover boy, Daniel. She would go out of the patio window in the basement, that was close to the ground. After the first week she was collected again by her mother, who had tracked her down to this place in Rhu. She was taken home. The patio window in the basement was now a well known secret.

After that we got two college students, Valerie and Fiona, last one was Scottish, and we could not understand her at all. She also was not specially interested in working, but she was tolerable. Valerie turned out to be the nicest girl among them. Very friendly and always helping us with English.

Now I am here over two months and still I get irritated at times when I am confronted by such laziness of some of the staff. It gets me mad and I have to leave the situation, so I won't blow up. I am getting tired of it. Erika is already making plans to go to someplace in France, same deal. She wants me to go, but I have to get English straight first, plus I want to go to America. It's Joan that makes me mad, she is hiding again, from her duties, nobody can find her. She shows up as soon as she suspects that the work is done, or almost done; then shows up, cleans one cup, or puts a set of silver on the table and that is it. She is the only one of the girls there from the beginning. She is the one with the black teeth in her mouth, so very young but such bad teeth, its a pity.

Since yesterday we have a new woman, Mrs. Renner, about 40 – 45 years. She is supposed to be a waitress, and to know what has to be done, so it is told to us. She is the fastest yet in all of her duties. She washes the dishes with extraordinary speed, with much noise, she drags the dishes through the water once and then with the other hand she dries them. It was Joan's turn today to do the dishes, but she did not show up. She was hiding out somewhere else, doing dry work, like setting the guests table.

We were watching this Renner lady, and noted that the 2nd lady did not correct her, unlike us, she was worried the Renner woman would leave and we needed the staff. So she kept quiet, per our observation. We were not allowed to say anything, because we were too young, and the Renner was older and married to boot. That would have been against tradition to reprimand a missus, not good form. Joan was now playing both sides of this situations. She agreed with us but, then she went and stuck up for Renner. It seemed they had formed an alliance. Joan did not like us, but since the 1st lady always praised us,

218

especially at dinner, Joan was powerless. She had to accept us. Joan thought that it was a shame, and unfortunate for us, that we were not born in England. However, Joan would be gone, lost to us, when work was to be done. She would always find a way to get out of it.

The final straw that day came from *Rumpelstilskin*, I had no reason to mention him much; he was so unimportant that one could overlook him easily. As I already mentioned he is small of size, skinny in appearance, that one could think he might collapse, if it was not for the dirt that stuck to him, it kept him from folding up; he was *"ein schmuddeliches Kerlchen"* dirty slob.

Lately we had discovered, or just plain noticed, some evil character traits on him. He was trying to feel up Valerie. He managed to get locked up with her in a bedroom. We think he did it on purpose, as she was cleaning that room. He came in, tried to embrace her and Valerie came running out, outraged, crying hysterically, and refused to work anywhere in his vicinity. Enter the Renner, who would make just about any situation her own. She took it on to herself, to let *Rumpelstiltskin* have it, with full barrels. She was pretty rough on him, but he deserved it, on all accounts. The management ladies were off the hook and did not have to officially deal with it. Mrs. Renner had taken care of that problem. She had no issues when confronting people.

Now we noticed that he did hang around us as well, at times, when we were alone in the basement. But we just laughed about it and we thought he had come into his second childhood. In general he did leave us alone. I think all of us would have done more than just cuss him out. All of us were a lot bigger and had no fear of this little gnome. He found little ways to get on our nerves, I think to get even. He would not give us soap, he kept the dry room locked and so on. Latest items was that we were always out of dish wash soap and needed to take the clothes soap, which he and Renner smeared over the washcloth, to thatch it up. We died laughing. Here we go with

Kernseife again (Curd soap). What next. But maybe that was normal for them, who knows?

So the days ran into each other and we keep on trucking. Renner and Joan had now gotten even closer; we suspecting that they are leaving the premises at night, climbing in and out of the basement window. There have been signs to that effect. Especially since the 1st lady had to open the big front door again, last week, under great palaver. We think the two are going to the Pub (tavern) in the village and meeting up with their boyfriends. Lately neither could get done with their work, fast enough to be able to leave; so we thought they had dates. We could hear them whisper, their heads together.

In time we found out more about Renner. We gave her a nickname, the "top lady," due to the way she carried her hair-do; it was styled all the way on top of her head. Actually the 2nd lady called her the "top lady," not because of her hair-do, but because she thought of her as "top-notch" and deserved the title. Actually, not so much.

Her identifying marks were that she was always made up, applied her make up almost like a clown. It seems that those that liked make up, put on too much. She also liked a lot of jewelry, long earrings and super long necklaces. She was really put together with a lot of ornaments. She loved very colorful clothes, especially those that had some glitter in it. She was older, had quite a bit of time in her face and she powdered her wrinkles with a lot of pink stuff.

Her table manners were not the best either; she too had false teeth, which gave her some trouble eating. The food would get stuck in them, then she just dropped them down, or she would put the knife into her mouth to get the food. One time she put her finger into her mouth looking for the rest of the food, then not having a napkin she wiped her finger under her armpit. Then she burps. That manner was done by the rest as well. With us not so much; it would have been an accident, if one would have burped and we would have excused ourselves.

She had five children, but was separated from her husband. Before she came here she lived with her boyfriend, who had just sent her some money. He wanted her back. But now she decided that she would rather go back to her husband, who also wanted her back. That is when her boyfriend called her on the telephone. He demanded that she return to him. If she would go back to her husband, he would kill her. Since the "top lady" is here we have new events almost every day.

It is Saturday, Susan, Erika and I went for a hike around the Lake. We went quite a bit out of the way. We just came in time to see a fisherman dragging a woman out of the lake. We ran over as quickly as we could, to offer our help. We helped to get her to a safer place, took off her wet clothes, wrapped her into a blanket that we secured from a group of boys that had tents up, near by. We sent one of them to get the police and an ambulance. She had no identification with her at all, no money, no name, nothing.

We waited a good hour before the police arrived who took her to the hospital. The poor woman could have died right under our hands, we complained. Sometimes she gave off some sounds, we thought she might be in pain. We thought she had tried to commit suicide, she was pregnant and she wanted to kill herself, why else was she in the water? The next day two detectives showed up and we had to give our statements. However we could not add more to why she was there, why she wanted to die. We never found out more about this situation.

It is a day later, Sunday. I am downstairs in the dish wash room, nobody showed up, again, it was not my turn, but here I am. I heard a lot of commotion in the other rooms and I saw Rumpelstiltskin and the 1st lady running by my open door, a loud debate was going on. I went after them and saw them disappearing around the corner with a mop in one hand and a bucket in the other. In the distance I heard a spectacle and a rushing sound. I proceeded in the direction of the noise and in no time flat was up to my ankle in the water, warm water.

One of the old rusted boilers had busted, it exploded, I was told, and the water gushed out with great speed, filling up the basement, including the dish wash kitchen. The entire basement stood under water. The linen room, the different corridors down here, even a few guest rooms, all under water. I rushed back to the steps to get myself to higher ground, to safety. Everything was floating, oranges, apples, coffee cans, some food items, in between toilet paper and briquets.

As soon as the water receded we went to work with mop, buckets and brooms to clean up, to save what could be saved. We went in with our shoes, no time to take them off. We tried to guide the water towards an outlet, which was plugged up, wouldn't you know it. We had to clear that first. We scooped the water up with shovels into the buckets and carried it outside.

Now we had no hot water, not for washing, not for bathrooms, not for anything, and no telling when it would be fixed, or when the plumber could be here to fix it. In the morning the male guests lined up for a bit of warm water for their shave. To take a bath was a radical thought and not possible, we all had to take a sponge bath.

Now we were all waiting for the plumber, even if he showed up, it did not mean that it was fixed, this was not good old Germany, where things would get done lickety split.

To take a shower was a dangerous undertaking in the first place, even when we did have hot water. One would never know what would come out of the sprout, it could be cold or hot, and that without warning or touching the damn faucet, while you were under it. There was no midway in taking a shower it was what we called a *"technical tiefflieger,"* or as we say technical challenged. It was a very old plumbing system to begin with.

Then came the outcry around the "top lady" and her paramour. She had boyfriends here as well, not just the husband and the boyfriend she had been living with. She was drunk. She attacked Joan, in a drunken stupor with a knife. She claimed afterward, one of the boyfriends had doped her, wanted to kill her, and she mistook Joan for one of them. Joan went crying to the first lady. Valerie who had been in the room when this happened, fled the room, then locked herself into her room. The first lady had to calm the "top lady" down, then managed to take the knife away from her. Renner insisted that somebody had doped her up. She was drunk, to be sure. Maybe somebody had put something into her drink, who knows? End result was she attacked Joan with a large knife. That was the first incident and then another one happened.

I found a belt in one of the guest rooms that was on the ground floor. I thought it had been left by a previous guest and took it to the 1st lady. I was told then, that the belt belonged to Renner, the "top lady," who had entered that room via the ground window, getting into the house that way, when she came home the night before at 2:30 am. It appeared that she was so drunk that she climbed into the wrong window. She meant to have climbed into the basement window, left open for just that purpose. In her drunkenness she made a mistake, got into the window of a guest room, climbed over him, lost her belt and an earring. The couple woke up, watched in horror, as she stumbled through the rest of the room out the door, into the hallway. The guest promptly reported that incident to the 1st lady. I found the belt when I cleaned that room. She had to tell me the story, but insisted that I kept it to myself. Well, I just told the other au pairs, this was too delicious not to be shared.

The "top lady" could not remember how she got back into the house. Naturally, today she is in bed, deadly sick, hangover, but she lucked out, it's her day off. Now she will leave, we don't know if she was made to leave, or if she is going on her own account. Neither do we know, to whom she will return, the husband or the boyfriend who threatened her.

Chapter 35

Three Months and Counting

We had a lot of work, the staff is changing constantly. It seems that we three are the most dependable employees, actually keeping this ship afloat. By now we have our job down pat, and we work hand in hand, everything gets done in time. The 1st and the 2nd lady are pleased with us, one can tell, they knew this year without us they would be in a bind.

My sweater and beanie are finished. I went on all the tours, the many Lochs, including the Loch Ness but did not see the monster. Been to Glasgow and Edinburgh and all the sight seeing there as well. I am still hooked on Dr. Kildare, will not miss a day, it's on black and white TV, a very small one, but I don't care. It's a wonderful show.

I am getting restless, I can tell its been a long time without regular entertainment. Erika has made arrangements to go to France, Susan will go on the Cambridge. I am wavering. I don't know what to do.

Then came the letter from Fred. He is coming to visit. He is going to be in Glasgow. He has a weekend and I am going to meet him. Have no idea how I am going to put that into action.

We have been planning my escape for the weekend in the 5th month of my stay here. We have to come up with a good excuse to get the weekend off. We are planning to switch work schedules and I will have two days off in a row.

Now what excuse will I have? I can't tell them I am planning to meet my lover, or for that matter my potential lover. My handsome young American soldier, my Fly Boy. After all he is in the Air Force. Will he become my lover? I have been thinking about him, what else is there to do here? Susan suggested to invent a family member, uncle, that is coming through to check on me?

"Well I don't know, because the staff will invite him here, won't they? What do I say then?" I responded.

"I could not say, no he does not want to come here, if they invited him, to stay the night? They might get suspicious," I said.

If I turn their offer down, they get their knickers in a bunch, or worse, they will think, something is going on.

"What do you think?" I went on musing out loud.

So we went on turning over a bunch of different scenarios, trying to come up with a good one. We had time, six more weeks, so I had time to prepare.

"I have got it," Erika chimes in, "we will say, you have a job offer! It is an appointment, your new employer and his wife want to interview you. They are in Glasgow, will take time to meet with you, for a new au pair position in the fall."

"So why do I need the entire weekend off?" I asked them. "Part of this is good, but I need more to finish this story. Lets think on it some more!"

We still had new guests coming in every week, and often we would overhear the remarks made about the poor foreign students, that had such trouble to get with their system.

More new staff members showed up, some with ruby red lips, pink powder on their faces, smoking up a storm and sneaking back into the house after midnight, coming back from the only Pub in town. The basement patio window was kept open from the inside, it was now a well known secret. I don't know if the Ladies knew it, they might, and just pretended not to know. Who would have wanted to get up in the middle of the night, to open the door?

The weekend passed without a plan. I had received another letter. By now they came on a regular basis, one week apart. I would answer them the same day, the mail man took it the next day.

I had told Fred, "yes I want to meet, but you need to arrange from your end, I don't have any opportunity. I don't have money for it."

By now I had written home, to Oma, asking her to send me money. I might came home earlier and I needed money for the train.

Our pocket money here in the house barely kept me in cigarettes. I had given up on my hair all together, I would fix it, before I was to take off to see Fred. Glasgow was only one hour away. Fred had written he would rent a car and pick me up in Rhu.

"Good God no," I had written to him in a hurry. They can't know that I am meeting up with a man. I will come to Glasgow, you can bring me back on the return, drop me off at the lake, close by the house, I can walk the rest of the way.

I could hardly contain my excitement, two more weeks. I had settled on the story of the appointment. By God, I barely talked one of the ladies out of taking me there, coming with me, to make sure I was okay, did not get lost. Little did they know Fred was waiting for me at the train station in Glasgow.

Oma had send the money and I had enough, if things went sideways, I did not expect it. Fred was more than okay. He had told me about himself. He was 36 years old, divorced, had two boys back in America, was stationed in Germany for another year. Thereafter he was scheduled to go to stay in England. We made plans. We were going to go sightseeing in Glasgow then off to Edinburgh, he had not been there, and it would be fun to see it together. We would stay overnight in Edinburgh spend all day and by the end of it he would bring me back here. I was looking forward to it. I was thinking in terms of making him my lover, I was very attracted to him. I made

 plans to beautify myself, new hair do, nice sexy clothes, let's see what will be?

The 1st lady only reluctantly gave permission for me to go alone, it seemed to be okay, to do the appointment, but she would have preferred that I would let another staff member chaperon me. Well, I talked her out of it. My story was that I was to meet my new employer and his wife in their hotel in Glasgow. Then I was meeting up, afterward, with a friend, who had come through. She and I would go sightseeing, stay the night, be back on Sunday late afternoon. Best story I could come up with, it worked.

The weekend came as planned, I went off to meet Fred. It was glorious, we went all over Glasgow, then off to Edinburgh, the castle, the place where Marie Stuart lived, where her lover got murdered, on and on and we spent a delightful night together. It just fell into place, I had a lover now, what do you know, just like that, I had a lover.

Fred made all kinds of plans for us, I just listened, I just wanted to be close to him. I told him I would try to get to Ramstain, when I got a chance. He told me he had friends there and I would have a place to stay, while I organized my papers for going to America. He had lots of good ideas and one of them was for me to get married to him. But then I would have to wait for years to go to America, I wanted it now, as soon as possible.

He dropped me off right close by the Manor, I only had an overnight bag, so it was easy to walk the short distance, I slipped back in the house, unseen, up to my room, where I crashed, I had no sleep for more then 24 hours. That is the price for a good time.

By now I was here almost 6 months and my time was coming to an end, I was getting more and more restless. It came to me, that there was no reason to stay, to finish my time, it was just short of a month. I still had the money Oma sent, it was enough for the train ride home.

Susan had an accident and was in bed recuperating. We had more work then we could muster, but we trucked on. The house was full to the hilt. We had ninety guests this week and not enough staff, they came and went at an alarming speed.

This week we had a young couple here, very much in love. We found them absolutely enchanting. He was quartered in the Bachelor's house, because they were not married. He would show up at first dawn to wait in front of her room for her to come out. From that moment they were entwined with each other all day, holding hands, until they got separated again for the meals. I found him the other day waiting in front of the toilet for her to come out, where he swiftly took hold of her hand, they walked off together.

I only have a few days left. I feel sorry, and melancholy fills my heart. I wonder should I have stayed longer? I went to the mail office downtown, in the afternoon, and somebody spoke to me right on the street, a stranger, to tell me they were sorry. The village was sorry I was leaving. I never saw that person before, how did they know? It seems word got around here pretty quick. "Did that mean, they knew about my trip, too? Had they seen me dropped off by Fred, a strange male?"

I will leave, next Thursday; I gave them my notice. I left it open with Susan if I would join her in Cambridge, France was out. I knew I wanted to get better in English and I was also thinking I might just go down to see what is happening on Ramstein Air Force base, where Fred was stationed. I needed help with a lot of paperwork. The thought to go home was there now, I had enough, it was time to go.

I still have to say that I liked it here and I was sort of sorry that it had come to an end. It was interesting to have noticed that I spent all this time here without any money, and I did not even miss it, that much. I hoped that I had gathered enough English as a start and now I would take more classes, until I got my papers to go to America. Also if I could manage to go to Ramstain, with all the Americans there, I could practice the language.

To get back to London was a rigamarole. I did not know that I had to make reservation five days ahead to send my suitcases on through to Germany. All things here are so much more difficult. The 2nd lady insisted she come with me, to help see me off, and a good thing it was, she managed to get all the right tickets and information done for me. In London I had to make sure I got on to the right train to Dover and would disembark in Ostende, once over the channel to get back to Germany.

230

I had a hard time saying good bye. Everybody was there to say good bye, I did not know that they would miss me, they said so. I never felt so much friendship coming down my way, so much demonstration of good will. They will miss me! Nobody had ever told me that they would miss me, not even my Oma or my Mother. Could it be that we Germans did not express our feelings, that we are the ones that were too reserved in matters friendship, or even love?

It did not occur to me that people could miss me. It was hard to leave now. Erika and Susan came with me to the train station in Rhu, the sun was out, the lake was very blue, it seemed, all had put on their most beautiful face to bid me good bye. I had a wonderful time here, I left with sadness in my heart.

Chapter 36

Girl Friday in Duesseldorf

Back in Duesseldorf, no longer at the AOK but working as Girl Friday, in anticipation of my leaving for America. I am still at the Reckmann's, but now I have Edelgard's old room. She moved into my previous room, which is lighter and bigger. I don't want a steady job, because I am waiting for my acceptance from the Norwegian youth group. I have applied for a visa and it's taking time. I am bouncing from one job to another. Now, all have these electric typewriters and I am forced to work on them. It's  hard to get used to them. Last week I worked as a telephone operator, connecting incoming calls from a central station to different offices in the building, what next? It was interesting.

I have to make my move. I am getting too old for the Norwegian outfit. I just barely made it as a student, extension on home economics. It helped that I was with them in England/Scotland. If I get an offer for an au pair position in the US, I have to take it.

Fred is begging me to come to Ramstein, but I have to make some money first. I can't just show up there, and then what? I am not planning on getting married, maybe he will wait. I have sent in the paper work, as soon as I am on the list and have a sponsor I will take off. It may take all winter. It's gray here, it rains all the time. Last week we had snow and it was bitter cold getting to work. Since my workplace changes from week to week, as a Girl Friday, I go wherever the agency sends me.

The papers are here, I was accepted. I Actually got an offer somewhere in Chicago, Illinois, already. I am dragging my feet, I really don't want it, not in a big city, I want someplace were it is warm, I want California, I know it.

Last week I made it to Ramstein. Fred introduced me to Inge his friend Ken's girlfriend who runs a bar. Well, there is my job, for the time being, and a place to stay. She has three kids, was married to a GI and went with him to Lincoln, Nebraska. It was a disaster, per Inge. She ran off, after having three kids, all girls. She could not stand it anymore. She went to visit her home, here in Germany, never went back; instead she got a divorce.

Actually, the bar is rather like a Gasthof, a Tavern, drinks, juke box, dancing, a little food, not much just some easy to make stuff. There were a lot of GIs hanging out every night, great opportunity to practice English. Lots of potential for new boyfriends to Fred's displeasure. He shows up every night, to check on me, or sends one of his buddies to watch over me. Really there was no need; I was completely consumed with getting myself ready, paperwork and all, practicing English as well.

Ken, Inge's boyfriend, was from Stockton, California and he was going to marry her, three kids and all. Inge trained me in doing the drinks, I was behind the bar.   There was also a huge Shepherd dog called Rex. You had to watch him, never leave food out, he would gobble it up. One day, it was the first Thanksgiving I took part in.

Inge made a big roast, left it on the kitchen table to cool off, while we set the table in the dining room, waiting tor Ken and Fred to show up. Guess what, Rex was left in the kitchen, or he got in somehow, same results. He got the roast, it was huge, he ate it all. When we came in the roast was gone, the plate broken on the kitchen floor, Rex in the corner with a very guilty face. If a dog can make a guilty face, it was him, he had it.

Well that Thanksgiving, my first, Inge called Ken and he brought a bunch of hamburgers for dinner. That was the first time I had a hamburger. The best I ever ate were the ones from the base.

I got a new offer, this time from Beverly Hills, California. I wrote an introduction letter and explained what I was willing to do. They did not want me. Ken asked me to show him a copy the letter I wrote the family and was laughing, afterward. He and Fred then told me what to say. In my next letter I had turned into this great German cook, lie, and this wonderful babysitter: had not babysat once in my entire life. I did not know anybody with kids to babysit, actually, they scared me more then the cooking I lied about.

Now I had a wonderful introduction letter and soon I got a new inquiry, this time from San Mateo, California, a doctor's family. My new letter went off and I was accepted. I thought how hard can it be to cook, I take a German cook book along, as for the four kids, well, I was a kid myself once, and after all I am a female. How hard can it be to handle kids, it should be in my DNA, after all I was female. Easy as pie. Not really, I found out later.

Now came the paperwork. *"Ach du lieber"* Good Lord, what I had to come up with and how often I had to travel to Frankfurt. The paperwork was substantial, in which I had to agree and sign, that I was not a communist, that I would never ask for public assistance, that I had to keep a job, had a sponsor, that I took all the vaccinations required.

It took two trips because I could not find a doctor to give me a particular shot; it had to be small pox, because afterward my arm swelled up. I could not move it for two weeks. I had to arrange for a loan with Chase Manhattan bank, which was to be paid off over the first 6 months, I was in the USA, with 65 dollars a month. If I fulfilled the obligation of a year of service I would receive a 300 dollar bonus from the family, which could take me back to Germany.

The family was to pay me $ 120 a month, room and board and I had one day off per week. This was the indentured servitude I had been reading about. Wasn't it? It was the price I had to pay to come; I was willing to give it. I had a full fledged education, a good job if I had wanted it, I was willing to give all that up, to come to the promised land.

After all that rigamarole I did get my Visa and it was not just a Visa, it was a Green Card. I just had to renew it once a year.

Fred was a big help, he would supply me with a driver, a young recruit to take me to all my appointments. Fred was a Warrant Officer; so was Ken, which meant they had a bunch of young guys at their disposal. I needed to go to Frankfurt for a lot of paperwork. The first time I went I had trouble finding the clinic who would give me the required shot. It was the World Health Organization, it had to be, come to think about it now. These shots were no longer necessary in Germany and that is why I had to go to a special place in Frankfurt.

Fred and I picked up where we left things after Scotland. We went to Paris together, on his trip to Belgium for the Air Force. It was a side trip to Paris and then to Brussels. He was doing more than hinting now. His time was almost up here and he wanted me to go with him to England. I told him that I had to take my chance to go to the USA. Now that I had a sponsor. He said "I know" I just want you to know, you could come with me, as my wife, if you want too. I loved him for that a little, I guess not enough to change my plans.

Then there was Inge. She told me, more then once. Don't get married to a GI, look what happened to me. I was in love, but after a while I could not stand that place he called home. It was a mistake. I told her, Inge, I don't want to get married, not now, later, maybe I will. I would not marry a GI to get to the States, I know a lot of German girls do, but that was not my way. Don't worry about me. I have it figured out.

"Inge" I said, " I have to tell you something, a secret!" "When I was on the trip with Fred, he told me he had a vasectomy, he can't make any more children. I think, as much as I like him, I do want children, at least one and he will not be able to. So what happens if in some years to come, I will resent him? We, Fred and I talked about it on the trip. First he tells me he wants me to come to England with him, as his wife. Then he tells me about this vasectomy, how I had to know about it, it would not be fair to me, to withhold that information from me. I was relieved that he had, so I would not have to be so careful making love, but when I thought about it, it manifested in my mind as a flaw, which I could not overlook." *It was a bitter sweet feeling that would overcome me, when I thought about him and me.*

Made in the USA
Charleston, SC
28 December 2015